I0159934

HEALING
OUR DIVIDES

HEALING OUR DIVIDES

ANSWERING THE SAVIOR'S CALL TO BE PEACEMAKERS

DAVID B. OSTLER

GREG KOFFORD BOOKS
SALT LAKE CITY, 2024

Copyright © 2024 David B. Ostler
Cover design copyright © 2024 Greg Kofford Books, Inc.
Cover design by Loyd Isao Ericson

Published in the USA.

All rights reserved. No part of this volume may be reproduced in any form without written permission from the publisher, Greg Kofford Books. The views expressed herein are the responsibility of the author and do not necessarily represent the position of Greg Kofford Books.

ISBN 978-1-58958-774-8 (paperback)
Also available in ebook and audiobook.

For additional resources visit http://www.bridgeslds.com.

Greg Kofford Books
P. O. Box 1362
Draper, UT 84020
www.gregkofford.com
facebook.com/gkbooks
twitter.com/gkbooks

_____

Library of Congress Control Number: 2024933767

I dedicate this book to the tireless peacemakers and bridge-builders whose efforts shape harmony in our world. While some organize in movements and coalitions, many toil silently within their homes and communities.

Among these champions is my mother, Barbara Ostler, who gracefully nurtured six children with unique personalities and perspectives. From my childhood, I recall her gently singing the peacemaking hymn, "Let Us Oft Speak Kind Words to Each Other." With unwavering curiosity and compassion, she fosters connections through all our differences. Her peacemaking is a tender imprint on my earliest memories and in the depths of my heart.

Contents

Foreword

Social science research confirms what all of us sense: We live in a time of toxic polarization, with society undergoing a transformation more rapid than any other development in human history brought on by new technologies and changing demographics. Fear of such change has caused many to both retreat to the comfortable and familiar and distrust those who are different—those who are "other." In many cases, that distrust breeds contempt.

Such a reaction is natural and understandable, and yet for followers of Jesus Christ it is something we must overcome. We are called to be the "salt of the earth" (Matt. 5:13), an image that tells us that we are to be deeply involved in the hard work of transforming the world instead of being removed and isolated from its activities. In the Lord's Prayer, we are first commanded to pray that God's kingdom—a place where His will is done—will come to earth here and now (Matt 6:10). In fact, for the earliest Christians, the "good news" about Jesus Christ was less about what happens after we die than it was about helping the Risen Lord bring about that kingdom—part of a new creation—while we are yet alive. That kingdom is made up of "every nation, kindred, tongue, and people" (Rev. 14:6), and its chief characteristic is that its citizens are of "one heart and one mind" (Moses 7:18).

There is no more urgent task for followers of Christ in any time and in any place than to build that kingdom here on earth, amid the turmoil and contention that is the more natural course of human affairs.

But how is it done?

David Ostler has written a handbook that shows us. As it turns out, becoming a peacemaker is hard work. It doesn't come naturally. That's the bad news. But here's the good news: We can do hard things. As David shows us through his deep knowledge of the social science research and his careful reading of scripture and the teachings of modern prophets, becoming a peacemaker can be learned. It requires a state of mind, a view of others, and a set of skills that each of us can acquire.

Latter-day Saint Christians have been given a special charge by our apostolic leadership to learn these skills because our calling at this time and in this place is to become peacemakers, agents of reconciliation, and builders of bridges of understanding. I'm imagining a conversation ten years from now with a new friend who discovers that I'm a Latter-day Saint. "You're a Latter-day Saint?" he asks. "Aren't you the people who are the peacemakers? The people who work hard to bring people together?" I can't imagine a more powerful witness we could bear of the divinity of Christ and our allegiance to him.

I'm reminded of a scene from the dramatic television series *The Chosen* in which Peter expresses surprise at a teaching of Jesus. "That's different," says a confused Peter. Jesus replies, "Get used to different." Apostolic leadership has given Latter-day Saints a new and different role to play in the world today. David Ostler teaches us how to "get used to different."

Thomas B. Griffith,
former federal appeals court judge
and fellow at the Wheatley Institute at BYU

INTRODUCTION

Becoming Peacemakers

In the October 2021 general conference, Elder Dale G. Renlund spoke on "The Peace of Christ Abolishes Enmity," in which he taught that in order to truly follow Christ, we must strive to overcome contention and to be united. This touched me deeply and brought to the forefront a question that had been simmering in the back of my mind for some time: "What skills do I need in order to eliminate contention?"

Two years earlier I had written *Bridges: Ministering to Those Who Question* and saw how religious differences tore apart marriages, families, and friendships. While working on this book it became clear that we often lack the communication and relationship skills to understand others and live peaceably in the differences of our religious and spiritual beliefs. And as I pondered Elder Renlund's talk, it also became clear that as society is being torn apart with division, contention, and anger (examples of which include responses to COVID-19, the 2020 US presidential election, social values, and racial issues boiling over after the murder of George Floyd), we again often lack the communication skills to counter and prevent this animosity. Families, friends, and communities are divided and polarized, unable to find common ground. People who are politically conservative seldom understand those who are liberal, and vice versa. Increasingly, it seems that almost any group is becoming unable to understand or sympathize with other groups. As humans, we have always had a hard time understanding others. However, it seems more and more that we do not even want to.

Many who listened to or read Elder Renlund's talk may have said to themselves, *I want to avoid contention, so I just won't talk about controversial issues*. I don't think that was his point; today's issues are too important. For me, Elder Renland's talk was a personal call to find better ways to address the many challenges that face us without further fueling hatred and contention. It left me continually asking myself how I can better follow the Savior and not just avoid contention but replace it with becoming a peacemaker. I decided to read scripture, the teachings of Church leaders, and the writing and thinking of those who have studied the topic. Soon, my library grew by a couple of dozen books, and I spent hours listening to podcasts and reading online. I tried applying what I learned while engaging with people who have different perspectives.

That is how this book came about.

After I polished my first draft, I asked twenty-two people to be beta readers. Half were people I had never met. They were diverse, with different political beliefs, coming from different age groups and life experiences. I asked them to read the manuscript and help me make it better by identifying areas that were unbalanced, that over-represented a particular ideology, or that might alienate readers with how I expressed myself. Two psychologists reviewed it to make sure I was clear and accurate with my explanations of how our minds work. All these people helped me see things I hadn't previously seen and helped me remove rough spots. I learned from the unique perspectives of others and hopefully made a better book.

In a similar way, I am a first draft. As I wrote and researched, I opened myself to listening and learning from others. In the process, I changed. I'm still a work in progress, and sometimes I am more successful than others. I often fail.

In our increasingly polarized world, we become prone to identifying so much with our political and religious causes and beliefs that they become an identity overshadowing all others. Conversely, we begin to view those who see differently with as villains and adversaries, and we label them with derogatory terms that make it clear they are the enemy. Some of us may at times find that we even enjoy the contention, with an increasing number unfortunately seeing violence as an acceptable response. Through all of this, we burn connecting bridges and instead build fortresses and refuse to productively engage with people who think differently. Sadly, these influences have found their way into our communities and loving families and between fellow Latter-day Saints. "The love of many shall wax cold" (Matt. 24:12).

In that same October 2021 general conference, Elder Quentin L. Cook commented, "In my lifetime, I have never seen a greater lack of civility. We are bombarded with angry, contentious language and provocative, devastating actions that destroy peace and tranquility."[1] In an understated way, Elder Renlund said we have "shown tendencies toward contention and divisiveness."[2] At the next April 2022 conference, President Russell M. Nelson emphasized these points by emphatically stating, "Contention violates everything the Savior stood for and taught."[3] These three prophetic leaders do not ask us to withdraw from the public sphere and re-

1. Quentin L. Cook, "Personal Peace in Challenging Times."
2. Dale G. Renlund, "The Peace of Christ Abolishes Enmity."
3. Russell M. Nelson, "Preaching the Gospel of Peace."

treat from discussing potentially contentious issues. Instead, they point us to the Savior, the Prince of Peace, who commanded us to love. Love is central, for on it "hang[s] all the law and prophets" (Matt. 22:40). Only in him and through love can we find true, lasting, and eternal peace.

Peacemaking may seem daunting and overwhelming, as it requires vulnerability and stepping out of our comfort zones. Sharon Eubank, director of Latter-day Saint Charities and former counselor in the Relief Society General Presidency, spoke on this in her October 2020 general conference talk: "This world isn't what I want it to be. There are many things I want to influence and make better. And frankly, there's a lot of opposition to what I hope for, and sometimes I feel powerless."[4] However, with the right tools and as the Spirit guides and connects us to God, we can find the strength to make a difference.

Perhaps the biggest fear of engaging in peacemaking is that attempts to discuss divisive issues may be counterproductive and may instead fuel more contention. Of course, there are times to be silent, but silence itself can drive contention and polarization under the surface and leave these important issues to those who are trying to further divide us. Unfortunately, our quietness doesn't stop these toxic forces from infecting our homes and communities. So while there are times when we should be quiet and withdraw from discussions in order to maintain peace, whenever possible, we are better—and the world is better—when we remain connected with others regardless of their beliefs. As we become peacemakers, we help, support, and teach others who are looking for a better way.

In my research, I have found people and organizations that are having meaningful and productive discussions without contention. In this book, I share what I have learned. This path is full of challenges; we will make mistakes, but we also will find more peace and a greater ability to express our beliefs and have meaningful discussions. Through this learning I found myself less afraid of crossing these bridges of difference and even looking forward to talking about them. I've become better able to make my views known without creating defensiveness, to give others an opportunity to express the issues that are important to them, and to strengthen relationships while being a more effective advocate for the causes I believe in. Along the way, I have also had to confront my own weaknesses and practice at trying better. I'm learning what it takes to better understand where others are coming from, to find common ground and learn together.

---

4. Sharon Eubank, "By Union of Feeling We Obtain Power with God."

Healing Our Divides explores four major themes:

Understand today's division. In American society, polarization and division are increasing and are perhaps worse than at any time since the Civil War. Our level of contention is approaching violence and threatens our institutions. Since the natural man is part of all of us, we have tendencies toward division and contention. It's part of our humanness, and it's exploited by media personalities, politicians, political parties, social media, and other organizations for their personal or organizational advantage. As a society we are increasingly setting aside the skills and commitment to live together in our personal, religious, and political differences. This, in turn, is tearing apart our families, communities, and country.

Learn concrete and practical approaches and skills to reduce contention. We can be peacemakers and better understand others, create bridges, and articulate our beliefs without creating contention. We can discuss divisive issues while building closer relationships and in some cases, changing minds to create better families and communities. Simple but effective tools and approaches that anyone can use are discussed. Becoming a peacemaker isn't some far-off eternal goal; it is something that we must do now.

See how peacemaking is part of religious discipleship and moral integrity. We can use our spiritual and moral values to bring us together to understand and love our neighbors, including people who believe differently. Most of us want to build a peaceful and caring society; indeed, we are called to do so. For many issues, we can find common ground and reasonable accommodation of others without compromising our values. Even when we don't agree or find common ground, we need not see others as enemies.

Learn how to have deep and meaningful discussions. This book is not just about being polite and avoiding arguments. We need to be able to productively discuss today's most difficult and complex issues. Key to this is understanding why others might believe differently and finding common ground toward workable solutions. These concepts apply to anyone, regardless of their political or religious views. Because readers of this book will primarily be US residents, the examples given from multiple perspectives and persuasions are generally centered around the United States. However, they can easily be adapted or applied to the most contentious issues that may divide us among those within the US or abroad.

Likewise, the approaches here are largely from a Latter-day Saint perspective because that is my community, and we as Latter-day Saints have a unique vision of peacemaking and an imperative to heal the divides not just within our own religious and cultural community but also with our brothers and sisters in the broader community of children of our heavenly parents. (For the purposes of brevity, the term "the Church" is here used to refer to The Church of Jesus Christ of Latter-Day Saints, and "Latter-day Saint" is used to refer to the Church's doctrines, teachings, culture, and members.)

As Latter-day Saints, our beliefs should help us reject the vilification and hyper-partisanship that is so common today. We are taught to become peacemakers and to build Zion and its unity. Our baptismal covenant includes promises to "bear others' burdens, that they may be light; mourn with those that mourn; and comfort those in need of comfort" (2 Ne. 26:33).[5] Temple ordinances bind our families together in eternity.[6] These ordinances connect us to God and each other, eventually uniting us in one eternal family. We believe "all are alike unto God."[7] Because of all of this, we are a people that should be most able to fight polarization and peaceably live together in our differences.

Thomas Griffith, a Latter-day Saint, retired Federal Judge, and member of the American Bar Association's task force on American Democracy, notes that leading voices in depolarization see "Latter-day Saints [as] uniquely positioned to be leaders in this effort of overcoming toxic polarization." He continues, "To hear people like that see, in our culture, unique strengths that we can draw up on, I think that's terribly exciting. And I think it's consistent with what our leadership is asking us to do."[8]

When looking at the contentious divides (or our fear of creating them), it is easy to fall into the trap of immediately placing blame entirely on the other, and so it is imperative to be self-reflective and to adjust ourselves rather than engage in a project of merely "fixing" the other. To help, there are periodical *thought boxes* directed to you as a reader to interrupt

---

5. "My Baptismal Covenants," The Church of Jesus Christ of Latter-day Saints.

6. For more information on Latter-day Saint temple ordinances see, "Temples," Newsroom.

7. See also Mosiah 23:7: "Ye shall not esteem one flesh above another, or one man shall not think himself above another." The restored gospel of Jesus Christ is expansive and encompasses all people that have lived, are living, and will live. President Nelson says as much: "Each of us has a divine potential because each is a child of God. Each is equal in His eyes." Russell M. Nelson, "Let God Prevail."

8. "A New Mission for Latter-day Saints—Peacemaking", *Mormon Land*. Griffith specifically cites Eboo Patel, Tim Shriver, and Noah Feldman as opinion leaders who recognize our unique ability.

your reading and pose a question or encourage you to reflect on some principle on a personal level. These give you an opportunity to pause and take specific ideas that you can apply to your personal circumstances.

Healing our divides doesn't happen alone; it involves a community. Think about others whom you can involve, regardless of which side of a divide you may perceive them to be. Perhaps join with a friend or family member to read along, considering the *thought boxes* together. We often learn differently when we discuss ideas with others and consider their insights. At the end of each chapter, there are additional questions designed for book groups large or small. The *Resource Guide* at the end of the book contains further questions to engage group discussion, as well as additional readings and links to other groups that are involved in depolarization.

With faith and effort, we start with ourselves, making the changes we need to make, then we extend outwards to those closest to us, our family, our friends, and those who believe in a similar way to us. Although we may impact the stranger, we impact those closest to us the most.

President Russell M. Nelson invited us to this work: "Brothers and sisters, we can literally change the world—one person and one interaction at a time. How? By modeling how to manage honest differences of opinion with mutual respect and dignified dialogue."[9] We are taught by Jesus to become peacemakers; we are called by a prophet to change.

Because this is a communal effort, as you read along, I want to hear what you are learning, what things are unclear, and what experiences you are having. In particular, share with me disagreements you may have or blind spots or misunderstandings you see in these approaches. Since we can't be together talking about these concepts in person, I can be reached at **healingourdivides@gmail.com** or through Facebook at **BridgesLDS**. I hope to respond as I am able. I would love to hear about your journey and what you have learned as you try to become a peacemaker and heal our divides.

David Ostler,
February 2024

---

9. Russell M. Nelson, "Peacemakers Needed."

CHAPTER 1

Peacemaking, Opposition, and Love

Building bridges of understanding will require much of you. . . .
Contention drives away the Spirit, every time. Contention reinforces the
false notion that confrontation is the way to resolve differences, but it
never is. Contention is a choice. Peacemaking is a choice.
—President Russell M. Nelson[1]

I have also decided to stick with love. . . . Hate is too great a burden to bear.
—Rev. Dr. Martin Luther King, Jr.[2]

In the summer of 1975, I went backpacking with a friend in the Wyoming mountains. We hiked to Upper Cook Lake, a brilliant blue lake at the timberline. The mosquitos were terrible, but the mountain views were breathtaking, and the nights were free from city lights and filled with crystal-clear stars.

In that night sky, I felt the immensity of space. I was a tiny particle on a small planet orbiting around an ordinary star in the outer reaches of the Milky Way galaxy, which is just one of one hundred billion to one trillion galaxies in the universe.[3] In all that immensity, I could sense a personal and loving God, and I remembered His words to Moses: "and their numbers [of the souls] were great, even numberless as the sand upon the sea shore" (Moses 1:28).[4]

Despite being a single soul among numbers without end, I did not feel insignificant. I felt seen and understood. Among all the grains of sand, I was important and known. I felt that God knew and loved me, and I wanted to spread that love. The night sky spoke to organization. Even in

---

1. Russell M. Nelson, "Peacemakers Needed."
2. Martin Luther King, Jr., "Where Do We Go From Here?"
3. "How Many Stars are there in the Universe," The European Space Agency.
4. Just how many grains of sand are there on the beach? As you might guess, someone has tried to calculate it. Dr. Jason Marshall, also known as "The Math Dude," calculates the number of grains of sand on the beach as between 2.5 and 10 sextillion grains of sand. He estimates that there are five to ten times more stars in the universe than this calculation of grains of sand. Fraser Cain, "Are There More Grains of Sand Than Stars?" If our star is a one in a billion occurrence (average), that means there are many, many times the number of souls than the sands of the sea. In other words, the math works.

exploding stars, black holes, and the crashing of comets, there is order. In the universe's vastness, our heavenly parents see, know, and love every soul. The paleontologist and Jesuit mystic Teilhard de Chardin must have experienced something similar when he observed: "Love is the most universal, the most tremendous and the most mysterious of the cosmos forces. . . . [T]he physical structure of the universe is love."[5] These transcendent moments are fleeting in our contentious and divided world.

Reflect

- When have you felt awe, wonder, or transcendence? Was it accompanied by a sense of love? Did your heart expand to include others?

No Contention Among Them

Two thousand years ago the night sky looked almost the same. Just like today, the people of the Book of Mormon lived in contention and division. They pridefully distinguished and valued each other by their rank, and their society was filled with disputations, boastings, and great inequality.[6] However, after the Savior visited them, they were completely changed. As the prophet Mormon described these converted people, "There was no contention in the land. . . . And there were no envyings, nor strifes, nor tumults, . . . neither were there Lamanites, nor any manner of -ites; but *they were in one*, the children of Christ, and heirs to the kingdom of God" (4 Ne. 1:15–17).

Elder Dale G. Renlund says of this time, "Do you think that the people were unified because they were all the same, or because they had no

---

5. Pierre Teilhard de Chardin, "Sketch of a Personal Universe," 72. Perhaps de Chardin was referring to what we believe in Latter-day Saint theology to be the Light of Christ. This is defined as "the divine energy, power, or influence that proceeds from God through Christ and gives life and light to all things." See "Light of Christ," Gospel Topics.

6. See 3 Nephi 6, particularly verses 10–14. Orson Pratt remarked that the time before Christ's arrival in the Americas was very similar to the world in his time. In 1873 he said that these conditions "resemble[e] that which now exists among all the nations and kingdoms of the earth—some lifted up in pride and popularity because of their great wealth, others bowed down in the dust because of their poverty, and class distinctions prevailed until this new order of things was established." Orson Pratt, April 7, 1873, *Journal of Discourses*, 16:1–8. I wonder whether Orson Pratt would think we live in a more contentious time today.

differences of opinion? I doubt it. Instead, contention and enmity disappeared because they placed their discipleship of the Savior above all else. Their differences paled in comparison to their shared love of the Savior."[7]

Consider

- When Elder Renlund said, "Their differences paled in comparison to their shared love of the Savior," can you think of groups in which you feel this unity, even if there are differences between you and others?
- Are there groups in which you feel a lack of unity? Could you ever feel this unity with any individual people in these groups?

Once a people marked by pride, contention, and violence, now "there could not be a happier people among all the people who had been created by the hand of God. . . . And how blessed were they! For the Lord did bless them in all their doings" (4 Ne. 1:16, 18). This was a remarkable aboutturn. This was not some theoretical nirvana; it happened and even lasted for generations over two hundred years.[8]

What made the difference? It was "because of the love of God which did dwell in the hearts of the people" (4 Ne. 1:15). They became peacemakers because they loved God and felt a deep commitment to each other.

Not long before this shift from contention, on the other side of the globe, a rich man near Jerusalem asked Jesus about his place with God. "Jesus said unto him, Thou shalt love the Lord thy God with all thy heart, and with all thy soul, and with all thy mind. This is the first and great commandment. And the second is like unto it, Thou shalt love thy neighbour as thyself" (Matt. 22:37–39). Then the great teaching moment: "But he, willing to justify himself, said unto Jesus, And who is my neighbour?" (Luke 10:29). Jesus taught through the parable of the Good Samaritan who rescued the robbed, injured Jewish man that everyone is our neighbor. At that time, the Jews hated the Samaritans and considered them inferior, and these sentiments were generally reciprocated. There was a stark and often bitter divide between their communities. Jesus chose a man from this reviled group not to just demonstrate compassion but to emphasize that our community—our neighbors—includes those we view as separate from us. Thus, through this young rich man, the Savior teaches

---

7. Dale G. Renlund, "The Peace of Christ Abolishes Enmity."

8. See the 4 Nephi 1 chapter heading: "The Nephites and Lamanites are all converted unto the Lord—They have all things in common, work miracles, and prosper in the land—After two centuries, divisions . . ."

us that our love should extend to all, and in particular to our neighbors that we might otherwise prefer to avoid.

Speaking of love, Muslim scholar Alwi Shihab said at a Brigham Young University forum: "We must respect this God-given dignity in every human being, even in our enemies. For the goal of all human relations—whether they are religious, social, political, or economic—ought to be cooperation and mutual respect."[9] Love heals our divides, crosses bridges, opens fortresses, erases disputes, and removes inequity. We give up envy, strife, and tumult when we have a shared love of the Savior.

Opposition

Being peacemakers and maintaining the healing love that the Savior requires of us is not easy. Our lives are ordinary and mundane, with times of difficulty and loss. We all have pressures and limitations, whether they be struggles with physical or emotional health, economic challenges, relationship troubles, crises of faith, or personal tragedies. However, we can grow through all these conflicts. "For it must needs be, that there is an opposition in all things. If not so, . . . righteousness could not be brought to pass" (2 Ne. 2:11).[10] Commenting on this teaching by the prophet Lehi, President Dallin H. Oaks adds, "It is opposition that enables choices and it is the opportunity of making the right choices that leads to the growth that is the purpose of the Father's plan."[11]

Opposition goes beyond the times when we feel things are against us. It includes choosing between multiple possibilities and consequences,

---

9. Alwi Shihab, "Building Bridges to Harmony Through Understanding."

10. This scripture is usually applied to either the opposition of good influences or the opposition of evil influences, highlighting our ability to choose and grow through personal challenges. However, learning also occurs through opposition. Academically, it happens by testing a hypothesis, which is a form of opposition. For example, Galileo opposed the commonly accepted idea in his day that the planets and sun revolved around the earth, instead creating today's modern understanding of planetary revolution around the sun. Most scientific discoveries come through similar oppositional testing. Generally, new ideas are created which are then tested in opposition to prove them. In this way, opposition leads to better understanding, scientific findings, arguments, and business planning. Typically, learning comes from considering an opposing viewpoint or idea, determining whether it is more accurate than one's current belief, and refining one's position or adopting the new idea.

11. Dallin H. Oaks, "Opposition in All Things."

knowing that making any choice means letting go of others. And we don't make these choices in a vacuum. Like the cartoon depictions of an angel and a devil sitting on our shoulders and trying to persuade us, there are various forces, including divine inspiration, the adversary, and other currents within society that influence our decisions. However, unlike the animated angels and devils, we are often unaware of these forces.

Some decisions are between pleasing alternatives, like what kind of ice cream to buy. Other choices are between painful alternatives, with no easy options. Choices always open some doors and close others. As taught by President Oaks, opposition is important to our spiritual growth because we change as we choose from the possibilities and learn from the results. President Russell M. Nelson illustrates this principle through the example of discussions within the First Presidency. He says, "Differences of opinion are part of life. I work every day with dedicated servants of the Lord who do not always see an issue the same way. They know I want to hear their ideas and honest feelings about everything we discuss—*especially* sensitive issues."[12]

All relationships include opposition. Because we each have different beliefs, limitations, and motivations, every relationship provides opportunities to consider another's opposing beliefs and learn from them. Such conflict does not need to be destructive; it can instead be creative. Whether at work, church, or home, we face conflicting and opposing ideas and choices. As we confront our differences, we find opportunities to grow.

Recognizing Contention

While opposition can be positive, contention never is. Contention is embodied in the negative feelings we have about another person. It is the expressed or unexpressed negative interactions with another and their beliefs that create distance or contempt. Contempt is at the heart of contention. It's when we feel that we are better than the other person that we are prone to assuming they have nothing worthwhile to offer us. Rather than seeing them as our neighbor, as a child of God, or as one from whom we can learn, they become an enemy and an object of pity and disgust. Contempt may surface as anger and argument, but it can also be silently unexpressed or cloaked in politeness. It's not necessarily found in what we say to others, but it is found in how we feel about them. As the social scientist Arthur C. Brooks says, "America is developing a 'culture of

---

12. Nelson, "Peacemakers Needed."

contempt'—a habit of seeing people who disagree with us not as merely incorrect or misguided but as worthless."[13]

Conflict is also different from contention. We can't—and shouldn't—avoid conflict, which is a natural part of opposition. Conflict can be positive, peaceful, respectful, and productive, with differences humbly considered. On the other hand, conflict can also be negative and contentious, full of animus, anger, and vilification. It is how we approach conflict that determines whether it is contentious. Without the skills to engage productively, we may avoid conflict and opposition entirely, yet harbor contempt and allow negativity to fester in our relationships and in society.

Contention corrodes us personally and destroys both our casual and most important relationships. (For example, research shows that the presence of contempt is highly predictive of marriage instability.[14]) When we feel contempt or contention, our brain says *I know all about this and the other person has nothing for me to consider.* We then stop listening and stop trying to understand, and we instead formulate thoughts and responses to dismiss their views. We may experience high-intensity negative emotions, becoming louder and more forceful, as if to portray authority or superior knowledge. Or we may clench our teeth and go silent. When we experience contempt, our natural man takes over, shoving away the Holy Ghost who then cannot help us see others as God does and cannot open our minds and hearts to consider their points of view.

Recently, I was in a rideshare car headed to the airport to visit family. On the way, the driver started in on a controversial topic. At first, I listened. As he got more extreme and started talking about stuff I thought was just wrong, I felt myself growing irritated. I asked a few questions but soon found myself caught up with emotions and talking over him; I told him the *real* facts and explained why *he* was wrong. I didn't scream or yell, but I left no doubt in his mind that I didn't value him. I offered him no dignity, as he wasn't my friend, let alone my neighbor.

---

13. Arthur C. Brooks, "More Love, Less Contempt."

14. John M. Gottman pioneered repeatable and statistically significant tools to measure the stability of marriages and the likelihood of divorce. He says, "Contempt is our single best predictor of divorce." See John M. Gottman, *The Science of Trust: Emotional Attunement for Couples*, 123.

Reflect
• Go back to a conversation with contention (perhaps like the one in my rideshare). • Did you feel any emotions that contributed to the contention? • Besides avoiding the conversation altogether, what might you have done differently?

While there was conflict during my rideshare, I was the one who made it contentious. I didn't see the driver as an eternal soul, loved by heavenly parents, with the potential for exaltation. He was my enemy. I was angry and disgusted with him and his beliefs. To me, his point of view was dangerous and wrong. I could have approached our conflicting beliefs respectfully, could have asked him sincere questions that dignified him. I could have learned how he arrived at his belief and asked him what might change his certainty about his point of view. I could have changed the subject and asked him about his job or family. Instead, I lectured him with my perceived feeling of superiority. It wasn't that we had conflicting beliefs; it was my lack of respect for him that created contention.

Avoiding contention should not be confused with eliminating difference. During the Book of Mormon's two centuries of peace, when the people had "no contentions and disputations among them, and every man did deal justly one with another," surely there were farmers who disagreed on the best crops to plant, bordering villages that debated water rights, sons who wanted to be carpenters while their families wanted them to carry on the family stonemason business, and daughters who wanted to marry someone their families didn't like—all the classic fault lines of human history (4 Ne. 1:2). Yet, there was no contention in "their shared love of the Savior." They had conflicts and opposing ideas, but they avoided contempt by choosing to share in the love of God.

Arthur C. Brooks summarizes it well when he writes, "Disagreement is just another way of saying 'competition of ideas.' The reason disagreement—properly undertaken—strengthens a perfect friendship is because competition makes things better. And disagreeing better, not less, is what we need to lessen contempt in America and bring our country back together."[15] Yes, there are times to be silent. Positive conflict takes time and energy. Sometimes

---

15. Arthur C. Brooks, *Love Your Enemies: How Decent People Can Save America from the Culture of Contempt*, 183.

we cannot or do not want to pay the cost, but when we can *disagree better*, we can strengthen relationships and come to better societal solutions. [16]

Reflect
• In what ways do you want to grow when dealing with difference?
• What conversations would you like to have if you knew you could have them without contention?

Difference and Division Are Everywhere

In a 2021 address at the University of Virginia, President Dallin H. Oaks gave "the most difficult address I have ever undertaken" and spoke on the division we have in society and our need to be tolerant and united, even in our differences. He told the students in attendance:

> I begin with a proposition I hope all will share. As a practical basis for co-existence, we should accept the reality that we are fellow citizens who need each other. This requires us to accept some laws we dislike, and to live peacefully with some persons whose values differ from our own.
>
> We must not be part of what Professor Arthur C. Brooks of Harvard's Kennedy School describes as "a culture of contempt—a habit of seeing people who disagree with us not as merely incorrect or misguided but as worthless."
>
> When some advocates voice insults or practice other minor provocations, both sides should ignore them. Our society already has too many ugly confrontations. If we answer back, we mirror the insult. A better response is that of the late Chief Rabbi Lord Jonathan Sacks. When he agreed to meet with a staunch atheist who detested everything he held sacred, the Rabbi was asked whether he would try to convert him. "No," he answered, "I'm going to do something much better than that. I'm going to listen to him."
>
> Extreme voices influence popular opinion, but they polarize and sow resentment as they seek to dominate their opponents and achieve absolute victory. Such outcomes are rarely sustainable or even attainable, and they are never preferable to living together in mutual understanding and peace.
>
> Followers of Christ also have a duty to seek harmony. In the midst of conflicts, all should seek peace. Far from being a weakness, reconciling adverse

---

16. Brooks, 209. See also Disagree Better, an initiative of the National Governors Association sponsored by Utah Governor Spencer Cox (Republican), a practicing Latter-day Saint, and Colorado Governor Jared Polis (Democrat).

positions through respectful negotiation is a virtue. As Jesus taught, "Blessed are the peacemakers: for they shall be called the children of God."[17]

These are distant but not impossible hopes in today's polarization. We have too few peacemakers, and their voices are drowned out by the ugly confrontations that suck up all the airtime and go viral online.

Reflect
• Is it hard for you to coexist with others who are different? Why? • Why do you think we need each other, even people who believe differently than us? Honestly, would the world be better if everyone just agreed with you?

Does Avoiding Contention Simply Mean Going Silent?

We all have different social, political, economic, and religious beliefs. Even within our smallest and closest-knit communities, differences abound. Since today's culture is polarized and contentious, our communities, congregations, and sometimes our families are profoundly divided. In the last few years, we have faced intense societal divisions about COVID-19, gun rights, racism, immigration, voting rights, and conflicts abroad, to name a few. For many, these are emotional and crucially important issues. Family members may hold different views and find it impossible to discuss them without contention.

The last few years have also brought an increase in religious difference. More Americans, particularly younger ones, have left organized religion.[18] Many Latter-day Saints families include those who no longer believe in the Church. Their reasons are sincere, often reflecting a difference in fundamental values. For many of those families, there is potential for contention whenever the Church comes up in conversation. Too often, families fight, argue, and contentiously testify at each other. Other families agree to disagree quietly, sometimes refusing to connect with or learn from the other out of fear of becoming divided further. However, others have found

---

17. Dallin H. Oaks, "Going Forward with Religious Freedom and Nondiscrimination."

18. Latter-day Saint disaffiliation has been reported through numerous sources, including Darren E. Sherkat, *Changing Faith: The Dynamics and Consequences of Americans' Shifting Religious Identities*, tables 2.2, 2.3, and 2.6; and Jana Riess, *The Next Mormons: How Millennials Are Changing the LDS Church*, 5–6.

ways to communicate effectively, even in their disagreements. While a quiet and cold peace is the best some families can do, civil and respectful engagement leads to healing and a better, more loving place.

According to a recent poll,

> Avoiding politics in conversation is more common than discussing it. Most Americans (71%) say they have avoided talking about politics with someone whose views are opposed to theirs in the last twelve months, including similarly high proportions of Democrats, Republicans and Independents. Avoiding discussing politics may be motivated by a desire to stay above the partisan fray, steer clear of conflict, maintain relationships, or form new relationships that have nothing to do with politics.[19]

While avoidance may be necessary in some circumstances, the eternal plan isn't to live in a mortal world free from differences. Instead, the plan is to lovingly and faithfully face opposition as we learn to fully love God and our neighbors.

How Divided Are We?

It is hard to measure dividedness. It includes not only our areas of disagreement but also the intensity of our disagreements. While some believe cookies and cream is the only true ice cream flavor, they rarely think less of those who prefer chocolate chip cookie dough. However, if you put a New York Yankees and a Boston Red Sox fan in the same room to talk baseball, it could just end in mayhem.

Many issues are low intensity, like ice cream flavor; some are medium intensity, like sports rivalries; and others are high intensity *political* issues, such as immigration, criminal justice, environmental issues, and tax policy. Some *social* issues have the same high intensity, such as cultural liberality COVID-19 responses, and what is taught in schools. *Religious* issues also can have high intensity, including LGBTQ[20] rights and inclusiveness, moral relativism, and truth claims.

Pollsters and researchers have been studying division, polarization, and political animosity for years. According to Pew Research, "the level of division and animosity—including negative sentiments among partisans toward the members of the opposing party—had only deepened" between

---

19. David Schleifer, Will Friedman, and Erin McNally, "Putting Partisan Animosity in Perspective: A Hidden Common Ground Report," 19.

20. Lesbian, gay, bisexual, transgender, and queer or questioning.

2016 and 2019.[21] Likewise, NPR reported in 2019: "Some 84% of people surveyed said Americans are angrier today compared with a generation ago. . . . When asked about their own feelings, 42% of those polled said they were angrier in the past year than they had been further back in time."[22]

This polarization has steadily increased since as early as 1980.[23] In a study of polarization in twelve countries, the United States has seen the largest increase in political polarization. However, six countries showed declines in polarization, including Britain and Germany. Something unique is happening in the United States.

In 2021, Dr. Rachel Kleinfeld, a senior fellow at The Carnegie Endowment for International Peace, testified to Congress:

> By February 2021, 25% of Republicans and 17% of Democrats felt threats against the other party's leaders were justifiable, and 19% of Republicans and 10% of Democrats believed it was justified to harass ordinary members of the other party. 20% of Republicans and 13% of Democrats claimed political violence was justified "these days."

Of special concern, the level of acceptance for political violence is approaching the levels of 1973 Northern Ireland during its most violent period.[24]

How Would You Answer?

- Do you think Americans are angrier today compared to a generation ago?
- Are you less able to talk about political beliefs today than before? Why or why not?

Many Americans across all political parties have become consumed with political ideology that cankers their relationships with others. As polarization increases, the likelihood for political violence increases with it, more families are divided, and fewer feel the divine potential in their perceived opponent. According to conflict resolution experts David Schleifer, Will Friedman, and Erin McNally, "A growing share of people worry that Americans do not know how to disagree constructively and have too many

---

21. "Partisan Antipathy: More Intense, More Personal," Pew Research Center.

22. Hensley Scott, "Poll: Americans Say We're Angrier Than a Generation Ago."

23. Levi Boxell, Matthew Gentzkow, and Jesse M. Shapiro, "Cross-Country Trends in Affective Polarization," 18.

24. Rachel Kleinfeld, "The Rise in Political Violence in the United State and Damage to Our Democracy."

fundamental disagreements and conflicting values."[25] We are right to fear that these divides are intractable, leaving us unable to work together to solve the problems in our homes and society.

These experts warn us about the effects of contempt and contention:

> Reasonable people, including those who do not particularly like each other, should be able to disagree on substantive issues without democracy itself coming into question. But it becomes difficult to disagree constructively or find common ground if people treat each other with contempt or hatred. Under such conditions, democratic problem-solving grinds to a halt, and political warfare flares uncontrolled. We increasingly find ourselves in this situation in our country today.[26]

Divides and contention are breaking our relationships. In a 2021 survey, "one-third of Americans say divisiveness has made getting along with friends or family more difficult, with only minor differences between Democrats, Republicans and Independents. Two previous surveys, conducted earlier in 2021 and 2019, also found that about one-third of Americans said that destructive partisan disagreements and divisiveness had affected their personal lives."[27]

God sees, knows, and feels our polarization and animosity, and it pains Him. After seeing a vision of God weeping, Enoch asked how such a powerful deity could be brought to tears. God answered him, "Behold these thy brethren; they are the workmanship of mine own hands, and I gave unto them . . . [a] commandment, that they should love one another, and that they should choose me, their Father; but behold, they are without affection, and they hate their own blood" (Moses 7:32–33). Today's conditions, including our contention and divisiveness alienates us from each other. And God weeps (Moses 7:28).[28]

---

25. David Schleifer, Will Friedman, and Erin McNally, "Putting Partisan Animosity in Perspective," 1.

26. Schleifer, Friedman, and McNally, 36.

27. Schleifer, Friedman, and McNally, 6.

28. Fiona and Terryl Givens use this phrase to describe an expansive view of God as someone who is deeply involved in the process of salvation, to the point that He astonishes Enoch, who sees the weeping God and marvels. This book deeply changed me during the year I spent doing humanitarian work in India, when I wondered where God was in the suffering of the hundreds of millions of Indians who live in poverty and deprivation. See Terryl Givens and Fiona Givens, *The God Who Weeps: How Mormonism Makes Sense of Life.*

Book Group Questions
• How do you define contention?
• Has contention impacted any of your relationships?
• What topics do you wish we could discuss, but can't?

CHAPTER 2

Spiritual Beings on a Physical Chassis

We need to see a reflection of ourselves in each other—our dreams, hopes, hurts, fears, and despairs. Otherwise, we all become strangers and foreigners. Our differences are often used as barriers to divide us, when they are actually an opportunity to enrich our lives. Dignity is a moral obligation we feel toward people, not merely a legal requirement we comply with.
—Elder Ulisses Soares[1]

Real knowledge is to know the extent of one's ignorance.
—Attributed to Confucius

As we commit to becoming peacemakers, it is helpful to know how our physical brains process information so that we can better understand the limits of our own thinking and the natural processes that influence ourselves and others to believe differently. Seeing how our physiology affects our views enables us both to better extend grace to others and to find positive and effective ways to discuss and live in our differences. This chapter examines the following four guiding ideas:

- Our thought processes are often subconscious, meaning we regularly act without actively choosing to do so.

- We filter and simplify the information we receive into patterns and models that we use to make decisions. These models are mostly, but not entirely, accurate.

- Our brains think involuntarily and automatically—without us consciously analyzing each evaluation and conclusion.

- Our individual filters and models—combined with different life experiences, genetics, and eternal identities—cause each of us to see the world differently.

As humans, we aren't just higher order animals; we are unique as a species. Latter-day Saint doctrine teaches us that we are divine children of heavenly parents. God created us and gave us our brains and agency—the ability to choose. Our essence is our eternal spirit that has always existed and has always had an endless future. Yet, we live as *natural men and women*

---

1. Ulisses Soares, "Foundations and Fruits of Religious Freedom."

within the biological framework of a human body, with all its constraints and limitations in perceiving, reasoning, and making conclusions. [2]

Even before birth, our brains create innumerable neural pathways to organize and comprehend the world around us. Spiritually and physically, we see the same information through our unique models, filters, and individualities, and with these we come to different understandings. Even if we arrive at the same conclusions with the same information, our brains use unique neural pathways and individually constructed filters and models to reach them.

A Little About Our Brains and How We Think

Scientists are just beginning to understand how the brain works. Different parts of our brains regulate our bodies, our emotions, and how we think and reason. New technologies, such as fMRI[3] scans, allow us to examine the specific brain structures used to sense, process, and respond to specific types of input. We can see in real time how our brains feel anger, fear, happiness, and other emotions.

Without us even knowing or thinking about it, our brains control digestion, blood flow, heart rate, and the myriad functions of our organs. For example, when we physically exert ourselves, our brains increase our heart rates to provide more oxygen to our muscles; during prolonged exertion, we generate body heat that our brains regulate through changes in our skin, sweat glands, and blood vessels. All of these processes happen automatically, without us consciously deciding to speed up our heart rate or cause our skin to sweat. All animals have these inborn neural pathways that regulate bodily functions. We manage these essential biological processes in our autonomic nervous system, which includes parts of our brains, our spines, and even the neurons in our digestive systems.

But as humans we are more than that. We have cognition, "the process by which knowledge and understanding is developed in the mind."[4]

---

2. Latter-day Saints believe that as mortals, we are subject to the weaknesses of the flesh, including passions, biases, imperfect perceptions, and other physical limitations. "For the natural man is an enemy to God" (see Mosiah 3:19).

3. Functional magnetic resonance imaging (fMRI) shows how different parts of a brain are working. It uses a magnetic field to detect brain activity by identifying changes in blood flow. fMRI can detect cognitive processes, including decision-making and memory. Not only is it used for psychology studies, but it is also used to identify strokes, tumors, and other brain disorders.

4. "Cognition," Oxford Learner's Dictionaries.

Our conscious cognition is how we evaluate information and make decisions. Subconscious cognition happens without our awareness, using patterns and models to make complex decisions and draw conclusions based on what feels right. It happens fast and outside of conscious awareness.[5] However, unlike automatic and inborn brain processes that regulate our heart rate and body temperature, subconscious cognition is developed through our experiences in and engagement with the world. For example, when handed a cup of hot chocolate, most of us will immediately start blowing on the drink to avoid burning our mouths. This is not an innate reflex; it is one we likely learned after previously burning our tongues. Our response is now automatic, and we do it without consciously evaluating the situation. We use this same process to drive our cars, not thinking about coordinating the gas pedal, brake, steering wheel, and windshield wipers. These actions are almost automatic and subconscious.

On the other hand, our conscious cognition occurs when we actively weigh the pros and cons of specific decisions. The choices may be as mundane as considering whether to top our hot chocolate with whipped cream or what roads to take to get home, or they may involve more important decisions such as where to live, what to study, who to marry, and how to live a principled life. We use our conscious reasoning when we analyze a math problem, write a business plan, or even decide which TV show to watch.

Conscious reasoning takes time, but subconscious reasoning comes almost instantly. This is why it takes about 0.9 seconds for a driver to perceive that a car has unexpectedly pulled out in front of them, and another 0.2 seconds to step on the brake.[6] In 1.1 seconds, the driver's brain has recognized the danger, formulated a solution, and told the driver's foot to brake and their hands to steer out of danger. If driving relied on conscious reasoning pathways for these situations, it would take much longer, and we would have a lot more accidents.

Emotions are a critical part of cognition. According to social psychologist Jonathan Haidt,

> Emotions were long thought to be dumb and visceral, but . . . scientists increasingly recognized that emotions were filled with cognition. Emotions occur in steps, the first of which is to appraise something that just happened based on whether it advanced or hindered your goals. These appraisals are a

---

5. See Robert E. Patterson and Robert G. Eggleston, "Intuitive Cognition," 5–22.
6. Marc Green, "Driver Reaction Time."

kind of information processing; they are cognitions . . . they happen automatically and with conscious awareness of the outputs but not of the processes.[7]

Our emotions provide values and motivation to our thinking. When we see a child fall from their bicycle and try to pick out the sand from their scrape while in tears, we don't dispassionately calculate whether or not to try to help; we immediately feel compassion and concern. Our decision-making isn't used to determine whether to help; it is used to determine how can we help best. Research shows that emotions are crucial inputs into the models that power our subconscious decision-making. We feel something and simply know what to do.

By contrast, studies show that people with damage to the parts of their brain that feel emotions have problems with decision-making. Some make poor decisions; others may just be indecisive. [8] Our hearts (representing our emotions) and our heads (representing our subconscious and conscious decision-making) are not separate ways to think; they are intertwined, and we can't function well without them both working together.[9]

Challenge

- **Think back to a couple of recent decisions. Identify how your conscious and subconscious reasoning each played a different role in these decisions.**
- How did your emotional values impact this decision?

Elephants and Riders

In his book *The Happiness Hypothesis: Finding Modern Truth in Ancient Wisdom*, Jonathan Haidt describes the behavior of an elephant rider to further illustrate the difference between subconscious and conscious cognition. Like our subconscious cognition, elephants are big, powerful, and very

---

7. The full quote is this: "Emotions are not entirely subcategories of intuition: emotions are often said to include all the bodily changes that prepare one for adaptive behavior, including hormonal changes in the rest of the body. Hormonal responses are not intuitions. But the cognitive elements of emotions—such as appraisals of events and alterations of attention and vigilance—are subtypes of intuition. They happen automatically and with conscious awareness of the outputs but not of the processes." Jonathan Haidt, *The Righteous Mind: Why Good People Are Divided by Politics and Religion*, 52, footnote 40.

8. Haidt, 39–40.

9. Latter-day Saints believe that revelation is best had when our hearts and minds are aligned. "Behold I will tell you in your mind and in your heart" (see D&C 8:2).

smart. When a rider and elephant go for a walk, the rider decides where to go and signals to the elephant. The elephant picks the path and arrives at the destination. The rider doesn't think about how to avoid rocks and trees; that's the elephant's job. When the elephant gets off course, the rider can redirect the elephant. If the rider gives commands that conflict with what the elephant wants, the elephant usually won't follow the rider's direction.

Elephants represent our subconscious reasoning with all our emotional values, while riders represent our conscious reasoning. So it is with our brains: we can consciously reason what we want to do, but sometimes our subconscious takes over. That's why it is easy to succumb to anger, slip up on New Year's resolutions, or think skeptically of people who aren't like us. Our subconscious is powerful and makes quick, vital decisions like avoiding a car crash. But it also makes simple and seemingly trivial decisions, like scowling when someone says something that we disagree with.

Haidt concludes, "Most of a person's everyday life is determined not by their conscious intentions and deliberate choices [the rider] but by mental processes . . . that operate outside of conscious awareness and guidance [the elephant]."[10] Neither conscious nor subconscious cognition is better than the other; they just have different roles. Sometimes our subconscious, intuitive elephant gives us useful, trustworthy information that has no obvious factual basis. Other times, we are able to make better decisions when our conscious rider is involved to avoid unexamined, elephant-driven decisions.

Reflect

- When has your elephant gone off and taken you somewhere you haven't wanted to go?
- What kind of decisions does your elephant make without your rider?
- What kind of decisions does your rider need to make?

Filters and Models

Our brains receive vast amounts of information—sights, sounds, smells, tastes, and sensations—and then use mental models both to filter out what is deemed unimportant and to recognize patterns from the

---

10. J. A. Bargh and T. L. Chartrand, "The Unbearable Automaticity of Being," 462–79.

information we think is useful. To illustrate this, science journalist David McRaney describes how newborn brains develop:

> For brains, everything is noise at first. Then brains notice the patterns in the static, and they move up a level, noticing patterns in how those patterns interact. Then they move up another level, noticing patterns in how sets of interacting patterns interact with other sets, and on and on it goes. Layers of pattern recognition built on top of simpler layers become a rough understanding of what to expect from the world around us, and their interactions become our sense of cause and effect. The roundness of a ball, the hard edge of a table, the soft elbow of a stuffed animal, each object excites certain neural pathways and not others, and each exposure strengthens their connections until the brain comes to expect those elements of the world and becomes better at making sense of them in context.[11]

As adults we have developed sophisticated neural pathways. For instance, we are bombarded with information when we are driving. At 70 miles per hour, our eyes are seeing a constantly changing world. We are looking for debris on the road, lane markers, exit signs, potential threats, and a whole lot more. We might be listening to our driving partner or background music, but our ears are also open to a horn honk or screeching brakes. Even if we are munching on road snacks, we can pick up an unexpected smell of burning brakes. Pretty amazing to be safely navigating a 4,000-pound car traveling at 100 feet per second in an ever-changing environment. All the information comes in through our senses, but because there is simply too much information for our brains to consider, our brain filters out what it thinks is important and ignores the rest. When something unexpected happens, our mind's model signals a problem. Maybe it is the sudden brake lights ahead of us, an icy spot, or a passenger telling us that we just missed our exit.

The subconscious models are so strong that sometimes they overpower our conscious cognition. To test this, Haidt created a study where researchers offered participants a sip of apple juice poured straight from an unopened bottle. All the participants drank it. A researcher then offered a drink of apple juice in which they dipped a certified sterile cockroach. Despite there being no doubt that the juice was safe to drink, 63% refused. When asked why, most could not give a straightforward answer. Some said,

---

11. David McRaney, *How Minds Change: The Surprising Science of Belief, Opinion, and Persuasion,* 62–63.

"I just don't want to do it even though I can't give you a reason."[12] Even though the researcher did their best to refute their concerns, only 10% of them changed their minds. For good reasons, the subconscious cognition was so powerful that subjects had a firm mental model against drinking insect-dipped juice, and no amount of conscious reasoning could justify it. The elephant (subconscious reasoning) made the decision, and the rider (conscious reasoning) could not overcome it.

This should not give the impression that our subconscious reasoning (our elephant) is anything other than amazing. Our elephant makes correct decisions automatically and accurately in almost all situations, which is how we are able to drive, walk, eat, and live our daily lives without needing to consciously analyze each bit of information that comes to our senses. However, these subconscious models are only approximate and are imperfect representations of what is around us. They work well for simple and routine things, but they are not comprehensive enough to consider all the information, possibilities, and perspectives for complex issues such as how to take care of the poor, create economic opportunity, or make sense of complicated religious issues. Since we are so reliant on our subconscious models, we are prone to use them with certainty, assuming they are "common sense" and therefore being unaware of their limitations. Unsurprisingly, others may have different "common sense" models that result in opposing beliefs. Thus, peacemaking requires us to be humble and recognize that no one knows everything. By working together, our differing mental models have the potential to increase the pool of ideas and possibilities and decrease blind spots.

Tip
• When you receive information that supports an opposing position, pause first and give your conscious brain a chance to evaluate whether the information is worth considering.
• In a discussion, be open and think about why this is rational to the other person.

---

12. Haidt, *The Righteous Mind*, 43–44. This research was repeated with other scenarios, including signing an agreement to sell one's soul after death and stealing drugs to save a family member's life. Haidt said, "[Subjects] seem to be flailing around, throwing out reason after reason, and rarely changing their minds when [the researcher] proved that their latest reason was not relevant."

How We Know Things

Our beliefs form over time, some with thoughtful analysis, others with little to no conscious thought. They come from our values, neural pathways, and mental models. With imprecision, we form our beliefs. So, how do we decide that we know or have become certain about something? Neurologist Robert Burton describes "a general classification of mental states that create our sense of knowledge about our knowledge." He writes:

> For simplicity, I have chosen to lump together the closely allied feelings of certainty, rightness, conviction, and correctness under the all-inclusive term, the *feeling of knowing*. Whether or not these are separate sensations or merely shades or degrees of a common feeling isn't important. What they do share is a common quality: Each is a form of metaknowledge—knowledge about our knowledge—that qualifies or colors our thoughts, imbuing them with a sense of rightness or wrongness.[13]

The *feeling of knowing* is an emotion or state of feeling, embedded in our subconscious cognition (our elephant). We feel comfortable when our subconscious feels something is right, regardless of whether it actually is. We have all experienced complete certainty in believing something, only to later discover that we were dead wrong.

Remember
• Can you remember a time when you believed something that you later learned wasn't so?
• What happened that let you to reconsider your belief?

Psychologists have studied subconscious reasoning using a technique called the Cognitive Reflection Test, developed by Shane Frederick. The test presents participants simple questions such as: "If it takes 5 machines 5 minutes to make 5 widgets, how long would it take 100 machines to make 100 widgets?"[14] When posed to individuals, many see a pattern and wrongly answer 100. However, when this question is given to a group of people for a shared answer, they always get it right (the answer is five, by the way). Discussing opposing ideas helps group members step out of their intuitive instincts, consciously reevaluate, and come to better a consensus.

---

13. Robert A. Burton, *On Being Certain: Believing When You Are Right Even When You Are Not*, 3 (italics added).

14. McRaney, *How Minds Change*, 195.

According to Burton, having a strong *feeling of knowing* (certainty) causes our brain to release hormones that make us feel good and satisfied. Without that feeling, we may try to resolve our doubt and uncertainty; we may even become curious and seek new information until our brain is satisfied. Then, with our *feeling of knowing*, we can get locked in and not challenge our belief or decision, since subconsciously we don't want to give up the good feeling of being right. Thus, Burton writes, "the feeling of knowing, the reward for both proven and unproven thoughts, is learning's best friend, and mental flexibility's worst enemy."[15]

We know very few things absolutely—such things as 2+2=4 and that an object will fall when dropped. Instead, most things we believe are approximations of some absolute truth that may be very difficult to prove. Religiously, the word "faith" is used to describe hope and confidence in our religious beliefs; we then express that faith through action—by the way we live.[16] Similarly, our political beliefs generally haven't been formed through rational testing and revising; they have rather evolved informally, based on moral values and what makes sense to us. Thus, they can change when we consider others' experiences and how they interrelate to our own values. Through this process our values usually won't change, but we may learn better ways to achieve them in our lives and in society.

We only grow through change, which includes changing our minds when we are wrong. According to organizational psychologist Adam Grant, "changing your mind is not a sign of losing integrity. It's often a mark of gaining wisdom. Realizing you were wrong doesn't mean you lack judgment. It means you lacked knowledge. Opinions are what you think today. Growth comes from staying open to revising your views tomorrow."[17] This is one way we experience growth through opposition.

Reflect

- Next time you say you know something, pause and ask yourself whether this is a feeling of knowing or whether you have consciously thought through competing points of view to arrive at knowing.
- Ask yourself: what level of certainty do I feel I know this?

---

15. Burton, *On Being Certain*, 99.
16. See "Faith," True to the Faith.
17. Adam Grant (@AdamMGrant), "Changing your mind is not a sign of losing integrity."

How We Form Our Worldview

Our worldview is everything we believe. Psychologist Alison Gray defines it as "a collection of attitudes, values, stories, and expectations about the world around us, which inform our every thought and action. Worldview is expressed in ethics, religion, philosophy, scientific beliefs and so on."[18] As Latter-day Saints, we see ourselves as eternal and all of humanity as family loved by our heavenly parents. However, our culture, genetics, and specific life decisions also contribute to who we are. For example, my parents raised me in a deeply devout Latter-day Saint home. As a man, I experience the world differently than a woman. I am white and haven't experienced what other races and ethnic groups experience on a daily basis. I have lived in relative abundance and haven't experienced food or housing insecurity. Being invaded by a foreign army has never been on my mind. I have never experienced physical or sexual abuse. I experienced the social upheaval of the 1960s as a somewhat oblivious adolescent; I was living overseas in company-paid housing during the 2008 mortgage banking crisis. As an adult, I have lived in large cities such as Washington DC, London, and Boston, but also in a small rural New England town with two paved roads and just 2,000 people. This all contributes to a personal but limited worldview.

In addition, my unique genes literally shape me as an individual by structuring my body and brain, both of which significantly influence my thinking and my worldview. A study at the University College of London, also replicated in other studies, found that different brain structures correlated with different political views of the world.[19] Reviewing nine studies conducted in six countries, researchers conclude that "the combined evidence suggests that political ideology constitutes a fundamental aspect of one's genetically informed psychological disposition. . . . Political ideologies are complex, interactive, and environmentally contingent."[20] Similarly, a Pew research team analyzed "data collected from a large sample of fraternal and identical twins, [and] found that genes likely explain

---

18. Alison J. Gray, "Worldviews," 58–60.

19. Kanai Ryota, Tom Feilden, Colin Firth, and Geraint Rees, "Political Orientations Are Correlated with Brain Structure in Young Adults," 670–680.

20. Peter K. Hatemi, et al., "Genetic Influences on Political Ideologies: Twin Analyses of 19 Measures of political Ideologies from Five Democracies and Genome-Wide Findings from Three Populations," 282–294.

as much as half of why people are liberal or conservative."[21] This doesn't mean we are born with a simple, genetically based political ideology like we are eye color, but the genetic aspects of our personality and emotional makeup help shape the creation of our mental models and point us in a specific direction. This isn't absolute, and throughout our lives we can and often do change those mental models and political leanings. However, by recognizing the role that genetics has in shaping our worldview, we ought to be more respectful of others' points of view since they are just as likely to be genetically prone to see the world differently.

Our genetics and life experiences are interrelated, and neither contributes to our worldviews in isolation. This is because no one has the same genetics, eternal spirit, or life experience. No one's worldview is the same. We are all unique.

Consider

- Which unique characteristics and experiences have shaped and influenced how you see the world?

What Is in One's Worldview

Our worldviews include all the mental models for our entire outlook and what we think is right and wrong in our own lives and in society. Far from abstract concepts, they embody what we believe, what we want for society, and how we see it best organized. According to Lee Camp, a professor of theology, these include questions about our spiritual values and beliefs such as:

> How do we live together? How do we deal with offenses? How do we deal with money? How do we deal with enemies and violence? How do we arrange marriage and families and social structures? How is authority mediated, employed, ordered? How do we rightfully order passions and appetites? And much more besides, but most especially add these: Where is human history headed? What does it mean to be human? And what does it look like to live in a rightly ordered human community that engenders flourishing, justice, and the peace of God?[22]

---

21. Rich Morin, "Study on Twins Suggests Our Political Beliefs May Be Hard-Wired."

22. Lee C. Camp, *Scandalous Witness: A Little Political Manifesto for Christians*, 4.

Such questions are obviously not limited to those who believe in God or affiliate with a religion; all of us have specific beliefs about who we are, what we want, what kind of relationships we desire, and how we want society to be. Our brains don't separate beliefs into categories. We don't have a separate part of our brain that holds our religious beliefs and another part for political ones. Beliefs are formed, stored, and revised in our brains in the same physical way. Thus, the values we use to evaluate specific issues in our community come from the complex interaction of our worldviews and religious and moral values.

I am in awe of how the brain works. To me, it is an almost incomprehensible act of creation and love. When I think about it, I take a mental journey like that night in the Wyoming mountains. Instead of seeing the vastness of space and the powerful hand of the Creator who formed galaxies, stars, and solar systems, I see His fine brush strokes in the minute details of DNA, neurons, and neurochemicals. Choice and agency aren't abstract theological principles but are instead gifts wired into the very structures of our bodies. Even with the limitation of mortal and finite embodiment, we can be peacemakers as we seek to heal our divides.

Book Group Questions
• Did you find it helpful to consider how we make decisions through both subconscious and conscious thinking?
• What are the significant forces that have shaped your worldview?
• Can people with the same spiritual beliefs have different political beliefs? Why?

CHAPTER 3

Through a Glass, Darkly

When I was a child, I spake as a child, I understood as a child, I thought as a child: but when I became a man, I put away childish things. For now we see through a glass, darkly; but then face to face: now I know in part; but then shall I know even as also I am known.

—1 Corinthians 13:11–12

When we see our own imperfections more clearly, we are less inclined to view others 'through a glass, darkly.' We want to use the light of the gospel to see others as the Savior does—with compassion, hope, and charity. The day will come when we will have a complete understanding of others' hearts and will be grateful to have mercy extended to us—just as we extend charitable thoughts and words to others during this life.

—Sister Jean B. Bingham[1]

Our brains take an infinitely complex world and reduce it to something we can comprehend and act upon. This simplification results in us unknowingly misinterpreting information and having an incomplete or distorted picture. Psychologists call this cognitive bias, and none of us is free from it. This chapter identifies different kinds of cognitive bias—and some ways for us to avoid the distortions that come.

Revising Existing Models and Creating New Ones

Our minds are continually learning. If we encounter information that is inconsistent with our current understanding, we evaluate it and determine whether to revise what we know. As children, we learn that the furry creature with four legs and a tail is called a dog. We create a mental model called *dog*. When it licks or barks, we incorporate that into our existing model of a dog. But, when we see a cat and call it a dog, others correct us. We revise our *dog* model and create a new model called *cat*. Now we know about more than one kind of furry four-legged animal. A cat meows instead of barks. Eventually we learn about species and breeds and discover that individual animals also have distinctive personalities and traits. We are always adding additional details to our existing models and revising previous ones to be more accurate.

---

1. Jean B. Bingham, "I Will Bring the Light of the Gospel into My Home."

Psychologists call these processes *accommodation* and *assimilation*. Jean Piaget summarizes this categorization: "The process of accommodation is in tension with that of assimilation. While accommodation seeks to create new schemas (models), assimilation seeks to relate new information to old cognitive structures. In order to develop intelligence, organisms must balance accommodation with assimilation."[2] Creating new models requires a lot of energy and cognitive reasoning, so our brains decide whether it's better to throw out the old model and create a new one, to use less energy and revise an existing model, or to ignore the new information altogether.

David McRaney describes the tension between *assimilation* and *accommodation*:

> We are forever balancing between assimilation and accommodation, because if we changed our minds when we shouldn't, we might become dangerously incorrect . . . we might remain dangerously incorrect if we failed to change them when we should. To orient ourselves properly, we update carefully.[3]

Examples of *assimilation* and *accommodation* may be seen in how a car driver may respond to two new and different encounters. Experienced car drivers have a mental model of what we might call a *driver's safety model*. We use it to make normal driving decisions, such as passing cars, braking at stoplights, and checking around us to know whether we can safely steer around potholes. Once we are experienced drivers, these actions become very natural, and we rarely think much of our normal driving tasks while on the road. However, when a deer suddenly jumps in front of our car for the first time, our brains default to that *driver's safety model* to act as best we can. We probably brake, swerve, and try to avoid the deer, stay on the road, and not hit other cars. After our heart rate has returned to normal, we might talk with others about what happened and how scary it was. We then take and *assimilate* both advice from others and our recent experience into our *driver's safety model*. If it happens again, our *driver's safety model* uses that assimilated information to try to avoid the deer. Rather than throwing out our previous *driver's safety model* because it didn't account for deer, we simply modify it.

Later, if we learn how to drive a boat, we probably activate our *driver's safety model* again; after all, the boat has a steering wheel. However, we

---

2. Charlotte Nickerson, "Understanding Accommodation and Assimilation in Psychology."

3. David McRaney, *How Minds Change: The Surprising Science of Belief, Opinion, and Persuasion*, 117.

quickly learn that while some things are similar, we need to *accommodate* a new model and learn that we pilot, not drive, a boat. What we thought was a steering wheel is actually the helm or boat wheel. A boat handles differently than a car, with rules of the water differing from rules of the road. We *accommodate* all this into a new *boat pilot safety model* and start *assimilating* new circumstances to make our new model more effective as we learn how to pilot the boat.

Because *accommodation* requires more brainpower, *assimilation* requires less, and simply dismissing new information requires relatively none at all, it is easy to see how worldviews can remain so persistent and unchanging throughout our adult lives, which may result in cognitive bias.

In the past few years in the United States, we have faced situations that we never expected. With these once-in-a-generation events, some have *accommodated* this new information into an updated worldview, while others have simply *assimilated* it into their existing worldview. It is interesting to reflect on whether the once-in-a-generation events listed below caused us to learn through *assimilation* or *accommodation*:

- Learning of George Floyd being killed by police officers during his apprehension for possibly using a counterfeit $20 bill.
- Experiencing the COVID-19 global pandemic.
- Watching the events at the US Capitol on January 6, 2021.
- Reading and watching news about Russia's invasion of Ukraine or the conflict between Israel and Gaza.
- Experiencing the financial meltdown of 2008 and the subsequent mortgage banking crisis.
- Reading about mass shootings in public schools such as Uvalde, Sandy Hook, and Columbine.

It requires brainpower to consider what the new information from these significant, far-reaching events means for our mental models.

Consider
• Think about when you were confronted with information that challenged something you previously thought was true. Had you encountered that information previously? If so, did you ignore it or assimilate it into an existing belief?
• When you learned that new information, did it change your belief? What made you change this time?

Confirmation Bias

Confirmation bias is a particular type of cognitive bias that favors information that supports our existing thoughts and resists that which contradicts them. According to Latter-day Saint lawyer and professor Lisa Grow, "A large body of research demonstrates that . . . our political beliefs can even influence the way we process information: we tend (subconsciously) to credit information that reinforces our political priors and discount information that contradicts those preexisting beliefs."[4] The same is true for any kind of belief: we are more likely to believe new information that confirms what we already think.

A classic example of confirmation bias can be seen in the 1985 launch of New Coke. Coca-Cola had done extensive research that showed this new drink would be a winner. Some warning signs and negative information emerged through taste tests and focus groups, but these were simply assimilated into the company's prior belief that New Coke would be a winner or were just explained away. This contributed to one of the biggest marketing failures in history. Confident in their belief that New Coke was a sure winner, the market researchers didn't fully consider disconfirming information.[5]

We can do this in our careers, religious lives, and families. Confirmation bias causes us to favor information that supports our existing thoughts and to resist information that contradicts them. When dissonant information enters our brain, we feel unsettled, and we decide whether to ignore, *assimilate*, or *accommodate* it. Since revising our models or creating new ones requires the most effort, we often naturally take the path of least resistance.

In politics, confirmation bias expresses itself in our being more likely to read or believe statements or media that reaffirms our position or supports our candidate, and less likely to believe those that challenge or oppose our views. We thus end up in an echo chamber, reading and watching political news that matches our own beliefs that further reinforce our biases. Patrick Miller and Keith Simon sum it up well:

> The more you talk to people who agree with you, the more confident and strident you become. People won't moderate their views or seek common ground if they primarily interact with those who are already a part of their

---

4. Lisa Grow, "'The Great Check': Reflections on Disaster and Faith."
5. Jennifer Clinehens, "The Psychological Failure of New Coke."

political and cultural tribe. The more time you spend in the echo chamber, the more you see "them" as the enemy.[6]

Because of this, it is virtually impossible to eliminate confirmation bias. A study done at Princeton in 1984 measured whether researchers could change participants' prior beliefs on the death penalty (both pro and anti).[7] Through elaborate approaches, they found that reading opposing information actually *increased* certainty in their prior position rather than decreasing it. They also asked subjects to weigh the evidence impartially, as a judge would. The results were the same, with participants' prior beliefs becoming more certain. It was only when subjects took the effort to understand the reasoning of the opposing view and to reevaluate their own reasoning that participants' worldviews expanded.

On complex issues it is unlikely that anyone's particular model has fully considered all possibilities. New information is always emerging, and with that comes opportunities to expand our worldviews by working to assimilate or accommodate new ideas before simply dismissing or ignoring them. Thus, the best way to overcome confirmation bias is to actively engage with people who believe differently and to consider ways in which our own beliefs may be wrong. Polls show "about three-quarters agree that it's a good thing that Americans have many different political viewpoints, including some that they disagree with. Most also feel that they can learn something by talking to people whose political views are different than their own."[8] If we enter these discussions looking for ways that others' disagreeing beliefs might be right, then we can get past our confirmation bias.

Opening our hearts to others is essential to being a peacemaker; this makes us more likely to connect and gain additional understanding. Latter-day Saint psychologist Jennifer Finlayson-Fife highlights this truth: "There's something really amazing about being in the room with someone you don't understand, but who you can connect with, heart to heart, and not get it still. That feels like the most Christian connection that genu-

6. Patrick Miller and Keith Simon, *Truth over Tribe: Pledging Allegiance to the Lamb, Not the Donkey or the Elephant*, 180.

7. Charles G. Lord, Mark R. Lepper, and Elizabeth Preston, "Considering the Opposite: A Corrective Strategy for Social Judgment,"1231–1243.

8. David Schleifer, Will Friedman, and Erin McNally, "Putting Partisan Animosity in Perspective: A Hidden Common Ground Report," 17.

inely helps you be wiser. Christian theology is that love leads you into wisdom every time."[9]

It is easy to see then that a healthy competition of ideas benefits us individually and in communities. Research shows that groups make better decisions when participants have different perspectives and can openly express their points of view. We make better decisions when we have church and family councils. In fields of science, including medicine, research is peer reviewed by independent scientists, which may challenge the confirmation bias of the researchers. It's why Church leaders sometimes tell us uncomfortable truths that can help us see things differently and may point to better choices. Individually, we can do this by asking others for input, particularly those with opposing worldviews (as hard as that sounds). Being humble and intentionally stepping back and consciously evaluating new information leads to accommodation and model revision, which leads to growth and improvement.

Try
• Read or watch something that challenges your opinions. (This takes effort, since the media we consume likely reinforces our own ideas.) Pause, then ask yourself whether you can see how they reached that conclusion. Put yourself in their shoes. • Lehi said opposition creates growth (2 Ne. 2:11, 15). How do you grow when you consider opinions that don't agree with yours? How do you stagnate if you don't?

Identity and Group Bias

Pause for a minute and describe yourself in your mind.

You might have described your physical characteristics—age, gender, hair color, etc. You might have described your personality—outgoing, courageous, funny, etc. Maybe you described the groups you belong to, like your church, local quilting guild, or running club. We label ourselves by family, generation, sexual orientation, career, hobby, political ideology, race, ethnicity, or national origin. When we attach ourselves to a descriptive label, this forms an identity. We have multiple identities, some of which are foundational and defining. The most important one for me is being an eternal being with infinite potential, watched over and nurtured in love.

---

9. "Belonging and Boundaries—A Conversation with Jennifer Finlayson-Fife," Faith Matters podcast.

Ponder

- "I believe that if the Lord were speaking to you directly, the first thing He would make sure you understand is your true identity. My dear friends, you are literally spirit children of God."—President Nelson.[10] You've heard this often—but give yourself a minute or two and think about it deeply.

- Now consider the opposite. What if you believed God was not a loving parent, but an all-powerful distant being who didn't really like you or notice you at all?

We all have a sense of self that tells us who we are in the world. This is an important psychological model that we form early. It grows and develops with new experiences. Self-identity is defined as "properties to which we feel a special sense of attachment or ownership. Someone's personal identity in this sense consists of those properties she takes to 'define her as a person' or 'make her the person she is,' and which distinguish her from others."[11] That last part is important, as identity is a model we use not only to know what group we belong to but also to label those who do not belong to our own. Groups are thus people with similar identity: families, congregations, left-handers, hobbyists, nations, etc., and we naturally relate differently to people within our groups than those outside them.

Because of this difference in relatability, we are more likely to be charitable toward and make sacrifices for those within closer circles of identity. Parents sacrifice time, money, health, and just about anything for their children's benefit, not even considering the return. Moving outward from immediate family, we might be quicker to make sacrifices for extended family, our local community, and our nation. The further out the circle, the less identity we have with the group, and thus the less we are willing to sacrifice.

Reflect

- Which outgroups are you willing to sacrifice for? Which ones wouldn't you sacrifice for? Why?

This can be seen in the ways that our brains respond to statements from those outside our groups. Using fMRI scanners, researchers found that statements by out-group leaders are less inspiring and harder to connect to than in-group leaders. They conclude, "The evidence we have presented gives some

---

10. Russell M. Nelson, "Choices for Eternity."
11. Eric T. Olson, "Personal Identity."

neuroscientific substance to claims that it is only when in-group leaders speak for 'us' that followers embrace their pronouncements enthusiastically."[12]

Another study shows how political partisanship affects the way in which we see others. The participants were asked to rate the attractiveness of people's faces in photographs. When shown pictures labeled with the name of the opposing political party, research subjects rated them less attractive and more threatening. According to the study, "simply labeling people as political partisans shifts impressions of their faces."[13] We literally see others differently.

A similar group bias happens all the time in sports. We often think referees and umpires disadvantage our team—even when shown replays. It is present in groups defined by race, national origin, politics, gender, sports teams, and probably everywhere there is a strong identity. When humankind live in small groups, they carefully looked for threats from outsiders; for them out-grouping provided protection. But this cognitive bias makes for irrational reasoning as we consider information coming from both in-group and out-group members.

Out-group thinking not only distorts our cognition, but it can harm us when it leads to thinking that diminishes others, blocking useful information, and creating contention and other barriers. In his blog post "I Can Tolerate Anything Except the Outgroup," psychologist Scott Alexander Siskin describes how the out-groups that potentially provoke the most extreme negative reactions are those nearby.[14] For example, if we are politically partisan, we are less concerned about the liberal in Oslo or the conservative in Brazil than those who live in our neighborhood. The strongest reactions happen near us. For Latter-day Saints, it might be the neighbor who left the Church, the family member with more conservative religious beliefs, or the fellow ward member who has signs in their yard for a political candidate we don't support. Proximity potentially strengthens the impact of out-group bias.

Our increased political polarization has led to an increase in partisan identity and, dialing up the intensity, even hyper-partisan identity. For some, this overwhelms all other identities and contributes to seeing ev-

12. Pascal Molenberghs, et al., "The Neuroscience of Inspirational Leadership: The Importance of Collective-Oriented Language and Shared Group Membership," 2190.

13. Brittany S. Cassidy, Colleen Hughes, and Anne C. Krendl, "Disclosing political partisanship polarizes first impression of faces," e0276400.

14. Scott Alexander (pseudonym), "I Can Tolerate Anything Except the Outgroup."

erything as a win-lose political fight. In their article, "How Hatred Came to Dominate American Politics," political scientist Lilliana Mason writes:

> With all these identities accumulating on top of each other, partisanship has become a kind of "mega-identity," with party identification standing for much, much more. In fact, it's reached the point that when you meet somebody, you can immediately size them up as a "Trump voter" or a "Biden voter." That kind of easy stereotyping leads us to see the other party as distant and different. And typically, things that are distant and different are also more threatening.[15]

This isn't the Lord's way. He doesn't consider our partisan identities; we are all His children. And in today's political climate it seems appropriate to liken Nephi's words to reflect that God "inviteth them all to come unto him and partake of his goodness; and he denieth none that come unto him, [Democrats and Republicans,] black and white, bond and free, male and female; and he remembereth the heathen; and all are alike unto God, both Jew and Gentile"(2 Ne. 26:33).

Concerned about the dangers of group identity, President M. Russell Ballard told a group of students at BYU:

> As children of God, we instinctively want to associate with each other. Whether we belong to a sports team, a musical group, a club, or other organization, being part of a group is often an important part of our identity. It also provides us purpose in life. . . . However, it can also be a distraction and hinder progress. Sadly, history has shown us that often we set up *group identities* based on false and incorrect ideologies that have harmed or marginalized others. . . . Marginalizing and persecuting people based on age, gender, nationality, religious preferences, or anything else can be hurtful and misunderstood.[16]

He then gives wise advice on how to break down this group identity:

> To avoid such misunderstandings, we must always remember that there are also larger groups to which people belong. . . . For us, the group that is most important to identify with is being the children of God. We declare that we are all the spiritual children of Heavenly Parents; thus we are brothers and sisters in God's family. We will continue to be a part of God's family after we die and throughout all eternity. Nothing can change that relationship. We must always keep this uppermost in our minds.[17]

Our common identity connects us to everyone.

---

15. Lee Drutman, "How Hatred Came to Dominate American Politics."

16. M. Russell Ballard, "Children of Heavenly Father."

17. Ballard, "Children of Heavenly Father."

Try
• When talking, consciously think about the ways you and the other person are alike.
• If you talk about someone who has different opinions and use "them" or "they," you likely are thinking about them as a member of an out-group. Think of one specific person and reframe to include them as in-group people: sincere seekers of good, a potential friend, or a child of God with hopes, dreams, and talents.
• If you reframe your perception of that person as a fellow in-group person, do you feel more generous towards them? Does that change your perspective?
• Consciously find at least one strength or positive attribute of someone with whom you don't agree.

Competency Bias

David Dunning and Justin Kruger, psychologists at Cornell University, studied how one's perception of expertise matched their objectively assessed expertise. Their question was, "Are we as smart as we think we are?" In 1999 they published their research as, "Unskilled and Unaware of It: How Difficulties in Recognizing One's Own Incompetence Lead to Inflated Self-Assessments."[18] The title says it all: some people just don't know how little they know. The bias has since been named for the authors: the Dunning-Kruger effect, or competency bias.

This competency bias also applies to skills. A study showed 68% of professors at a university thought they were in the top 25% of all university teachers. Another survey showed 42% of software engineers thought they were among the top 5% of their coworkers.[19] In these examples the math just doesn't work. It occurs in our community when so many people think they are experts on all political issues, including immigration, poverty, racism, election security, and COVID-19.

The reality is that we generally just don't know as much as we think we do. If we are smart and at the top of our fields, our competency bias might be even worse. David McRaney says of competency bias,

---

18. Justin Kruger and David Dunning, "Unskilled and Unaware of It: How Difficulties in Recognizing One's Own Incompetence Lead to Inflated Self-assessments," 1121–34.

19. "9 Dunning-Kruger Effect Examples in Real Life," Studious Guy.

The research on this is clear, the more intelligent you are, and the more educated, the more data at your disposal, the better you become at rationalizing and justifying your existing beliefs and attitudes, regardless of their accuracy or harmfulness. Basically, when motivated to find supporting evidence, that's all we look for.[20]

In a very real way, when we are learned, we think we are wise. But our wisdom is foolishness and it profiteth us not (2 Ne. 9:28).[21]

Much of today's contention comes from people seeing things only from their own perspective and worldview, either unaware, uninterested, or simply unaccepting of the validity of the worldview of others. Morgan Housel says, "Your personal experiences . . . make up maybe 0.00000001% of what's happened in the world, but maybe 80% of how you think the world works."[22] We know little about others' lives and the challenges they face. And vice versa, we overestimate our knowledge about the world, how others think, and the complex issues of modernity.

Challenge

- Think about an issue you feel strongly about. Now categorize your knowing about that issue into those three categories: things I know I don't know, things I think I know, and things I know I know.
- What surprises you about this thought experiment?

Some call competency bias a double curse: we not only misjudge our competency, but we are also completely unaware of our lack of competency, so we don't know to correct it. When left unexamined and unchallenged, our models or beliefs feel increasingly right, and so we grow overconfident in our competency. For millennia, people believed the earth was flat and the sun moved around the earth. To them it was completely obvious. They could observe the proof every single day. Early proposals to the contrary were often met with cynicism, mockery, and even punishment. Elder Dieter F. Uchtdorf put all of this in religious terms. He says, "How often has the Holy Spirit tried to tell us something we needed to know but couldn't get past the massive iron gate of what we thought we already knew?"[23]

---

20. McRaney, *How Minds Change*, 184.

21. Edited for context.

22. Morgan Housel, *The Psychology of Money: Timeless Lessons on Wealth, Greed, and Happiness*.

23. Dieter F. Uchtdorf, "Acting on the Truths of the Gospel of Jesus Christ."

<table>
<tr><td colspan="1" align="center">***Try***</td></tr>
</table>

- Cultivate a beginner's mind, a concept from Zen Buddhism that encourages "humility, openness, and curiosity." Imagine you're hearing or seeing something for the first time. What are you curious about?
- Ask yourself, "Why am I so confident about my opinions? What have experts studied that I haven't?"
- In what areas am I actually an expert? Everyone knows something, even though no one knows everything.

Like all other forms of bias, being aware helps mitigate this tendency. One skill is stepping back to question whether you have the skill and experience to claim understanding and competency. Another is recognizing and accepting that we do not and cannot know everything. We all are highly competent in something, but no one, not even the smartest and most capable person, is competent in all things.

Emotional Bias

Emotions, especially strong ones including love, cynicism, desire, anger, and fear, are important parts of our subconscious thinking. They help us act in the face of danger, marry and create eternal families, and correct mistakes in ourselves and wrongs in society. The more intense the emotion, the greater the impact.

Our emotions usually serve us well, but to overcome contention we must be aware that sometimes our emotions distort our cognition, resulting in actions and decisions we regret or beliefs we later learn were wrong. Most of us can probably remember a time when we felt strong emotions and created contention or said something that we later regretted. We look back and say to ourselves, "Why did I think that was a good idea?"

Generally, in conversations and discussions, strong emotions overwhelm our ability to listen to others, extend dignity to those with different beliefs, and reconsider our own beliefs and positions. If we can recognize these strong emotions, we can find ways to defuse any negative effects on both our thinking and interpersonal discussions. (Chapter 7 includes practices that we can use to eliminate some of the bias associated with strong emotions.)

Confidence Bias

Not only do we overrate our own knowledge about a particular area, we also tend to accept beliefs from those who express them with confidence. For example, when playing a trivia game we often defer to the person on our team who is sure they know the answer. Neuroscientists have studied this tendency and have found that just like in-group bias, we use a different region of our brain when we perceive someone as highly confident and accept their opinion more readily: "The findings anatomically . . . provide biological insight into the social transmission of preference and reassurance gained from the confidence of others. . . . These results also provide insight into the observational learning process by which someone else's confidence can sway and reassure our choices."[24]

Adam Grant, an organizational psychologist, warns us about confidence bias when he says, "We pay too much attention to the most confident voices—and too little attention to the most thoughtful ones. Certainty is not a sign of credibility. Speaking assertively is not a substitute for thinking deeply. It's better to learn from complex thinkers than smooth talkers."[25] Likewise, Brian McLaren, a Christian pastor, notes that we are "attracted to confidence, even if it is false. [We] often prefer the bold lie to the hesitant truth."[26] Grant and McLaren both caution us to be wary of those who seem to have all the answers, exude a level of confidence beyond their training, and tell us to follow unquestioningly. Instead of increasing our knowledge and awareness, they instead dominate with loud and commanding voices, cannot take criticism, and are unwilling to listen to different opinions—all the while unreflective and unaware of their limitations.

Reflect

- Can I listen to someone who isn't polished and still find insight and understanding?
- Whose voices are attractive to me, just because they appear confident?

---

24. Daniel Campbell-Meiklejohn, Arndis Simonsen, Chris D. Frith, and Nathaniel D. Daw, "Independent Neural Computation of Value from Other People's Confidence," 673–684.

25. Adam Grant (@AdamMGrant), "We pay too much attention to the most confident voices."

26. Brian McLaren, "Learning How to See, Recognizing Our Biases."

Contact Bias

We form our worldviews based on our personal and limited experience. Although we can and should strive to vicariously incorporate the experiences of others, we can never fully nor sufficiently understand the issues they face. Our different life experiences, biological factors, and circumstances mean that we cannot experience things as others experience them. When we forget that we can never truly understand other people and their experiences and worldviews, we irrationally make assumptions, which results in contact bias.

At the time of this book, wars are raging in Ukraine and in Israel/Palestine, contributing to global realignment. There is no way for me to fully consider what life is like for those living under the constant threat of violence and death. I see pictures of mothers tightly holding their babies while fleeing military bombing or pictures of a schoolteacher kissing goodbye their loved one who is leaving to learn how to operate a missile defense system. I can never truly understand the terror and suffering of both the innocent victims and those enlisted to fight. When I consider their circumstances, I suffer contact bias because I am not in their shoes. I may think I have some answers or ideas on how to address the situation, but they will be different from those who are in it.

Closer to home, I don't truly understand the experiences of people who face food or housing insecurity, although I try. The saying goes, "Before you judge a man, walk a mile in his shoes,"[27] yet we inevitably make judgments about others when we haven't walked a single step in their shoes. We don't just do this for strangers; we do the same for those close to us. Although I married Rachelle forty-four years ago, I have never walked in her shoes. I'm not a woman, have never born a child, nor have I been involved in a near constant world of unpaid care. I don't have her perspectives. My perceptions involving others are always incomplete and inaccurate. To help overcome contact bias, we can ask others to explain how they see the world. We can identify groups that experience issues differently and dignify the way that explains their beliefs. But even then, we must always be aware that we simply cannot fully understand what others experience.

---

27. According to AAA Native Arts, the first time this phrase appeared in written form is a poem written by Mary T. Lathrap. The original title was "Judge Softly."

Challenge

- Think about an issue that matters to you (immigration, education, healthcare access, anything). Imagine yourself in the shoes of the refugee, child in school, person seeking healthcare, or any person affected by the issue you chose. Think about their life, their hopes, their fears, their dreams, their past, their future—imagine them as being just as fully human as yourself. Give the imaginary person a name.
- See if you can speak as they would about the issue. Imagine their story.

Conspiratorial Predisposition

Conspiracy is when people act in secret to do something unlawful or harmful. A conspiracy theory is a belief that some event is the result of a secret agreement between individuals or groups, often to gain political or economic power. For example, in the 1920s during Prohibition, some believed a conspiracy theory that the government was poisoning alcohol to keep them from drinking. Since bootleg alcohol was often produced from industrial alcohol, the theory was that the government was making manufacturers add poisons to discourage bootleg use. Sounds ridiculous, right? Well, it turns out it was true, and thousands likely died.[28] There have always been conspiracies and their associated theories. Some have been proven true, such as the one from Prohibition, but many are far from the truth.

Because conspiracies can and do occur on occasion, we are all prone to believe in a few theories. However, some people have what I call a conspiratorial predisposition and are more likely to frequently see conspiracies in world and local events. Joseph Ushinski, a political scientist who specializes in conspiracy theory, says this disposition is characterized by "a bias against powerful actors that leads people to accuse those actors of collusion. . . . Citizens interpret events and circumstances with their underlying political predispositions such as partisanship and political ideology."[29] Such conspiratorial thinking is found in all political persuasions.

When people lose trust in institutions such as government, business, and religion, they become more prone to believe conspiracy theories. At the same time, conspiracy theories contribute to lower levels of trust. This becomes self-reinforcing and "can produce political disengagement, violent political reactions, and even lower people's intention to vote after ex-

---

28. Matthew Brown, "Fact check: It's true, U.S. government poisoned some alcohol during Prohibition."

29. Joseph E. Uscinski, *Conspiracy Theories and the People Who Believe Them*, 50–51.

posure to a conspiracy theory about government."[30] As institutional trust has declined, it is unsurprising to see belief in such theories on the rise, making it harder to discuss today's important issues.[31]

Additional Forms of Bias

Besides the various biases discussed above, other kinds include:

- **Community bias**—difficulty in seeing anything that might get us in trouble with the group to which we belong.

- **Cash bias**—evaluating claims based on how they affect our income or spending.

- **Catastrophe bias**—seeing things that seem immediately and disastrously dangerous while remaining ignorant of dangerous changes that come slowly.

These aren't the only forms of bias, but they all function roughly the same. When we encounter new information we may *accommodate* it through the development of new models, *assimilate* it without changing our models, or ignore or dismiss it. Our biases will always play a role in how we respond to the new information. A recent study shows that bias "can be traced back to the combination of a fundamental prior belief and humans' tendency toward belief-consistent information processing."[32] Specific beliefs that form the conditions for bias are identified:

- **My experiences are a reasonable reference.** We are only able to access our own worldview and assume other's intentions are similar to ours.

- **I make correct assessments about the world.** We fail to see the limitations in our own thinking and overestimate the limitations we perceive in others.

- **I am good.** We overestimate our abilities and minimize our faults while highlighting others' errors.

---

30. Silvia Mari, et al., "Conspiracy Theories and Institutional Trust: Examining the Role of Uncertainty Avoidance and Active Social Media Use," 279.

31. See chapter 7 for tools for dealing with conspiratorial beliefs. See also the *Resource Guide* at the end of this book for more information about the psychology and effects of conspiracy theories.

32. Aileen Oeberst and Roland Imhoff, "Toward Parsimony in Bias Research: A Proposed Common Framework of Belief-Consistent Information Processing for a Set of Biases."

- **My group is good and a reasonable reference.** We judge our groups more favorably than others'.

- **People's attributes shape outcomes instead of context.** We overly blame individuals for negative outcomes and reward them for positive outcomes while minimizing the effects of the environment or randomness.[33] That is, we may take credit or assign blame when the actual cause may be unrelated.

Despite these biases, our brains are amazing and can reliably think through many complex and important tasks. As with other subconscious reasoning, biases may benefit us before being able to fully examine a situation or issues. For example, in some circumstances, it may be beneficial to be wary of outsiders. In prior times, people from other villages or towns might have raided us, taken our food, and killed or enslaved us, and today we teach our children to be cautious around strangers. However, while they may be initially helpful, it is important to utilize our cognitive ability so that with time and practice we can supplant our biases with more rigorous, humble, and contemplative mental models, rather than allowing our biases to stay in control. As we encounter new and potentially contentious ideas and people, we can thus be more open and less subject to these limiting forms of bias.

Reflect

- Think about a person you have disagreed with over a particular issue. If you discussed this issue, which of your biases would affect your discussion?

We can rise above our physically cognitive limitations and experience moments when we "see things as they really are"[34] with the help of the Spirit, particularly about eternal truths (Jacob 4:13). But we mostly use our physically limited mortal brains and peer "through a glass, darkly," holding onto many "childish things" (1 Cor. 13:11–12). Because of bias, holding different world views, and our brains' physical limitations, we have differences that can lead to distrust and contention.

---

33. Oeberst and Imhoff, table 1.

34. "Each of us should evaluate our temporal and spiritual priorities sincerely and prayerfully to identify the things in our lives that may impede the bounteous blessings that Heavenly Father and the Savior are willing to bestow upon us. And surely the Holy Ghost will help us see ourselves as we really are." David A. Bednar, "Put on Thy Strength, O Zion."

Bridge-building is so important: we always have gaps in perception, but when we are aware of our biases, we can overcome them to gain a better understanding of others and to consider what they say. As the next chapter explains, certain forces purposefully prey upon these limitations and create contention.

Book Group Questions
• Can you identify something that caused you to substantially change your worldview? • Which bias was most interesting to you? • Which bias do you think most affects you? Which bias most affects the people or groups you associate with?

CHAPTER 4

To Act and Be Acted Upon

This life provides many causes for disunity and strife. Evil forces are working relentlessly to have us bring contention into our homes over any issue and threaten our happiness, our peace, and our love for each other.
—Sister Ardeth G. Kapp[1]

Anger never persuades. Hostility builds no one. Contention never leads to inspired solutions.
—President Russell M. Nelson[2]

Most of us want to be peacemakers and want to be free of the divisions in today's society, but too often we may instead feel like we are a boat on the ocean; we may have an engine and the fuel to travel, but the tides, winds, and storms leave us tossing to and fro. With all the animosity in society, the "tempest is raging . . . [on] the storm-tossed sea [by] demons, or men, or whatever it be."[3] These forces can easily push us off course. We yearn for the Master to free us by saying, "Peace, be still" (Mark 4:9). But, alas, we are human and live in the buffeting of today's world.

Chapter 1 described how love and contention cannot coexist and how productively facing opposing ideas and beliefs leads to growth. Chapters 2 and 3 focused on how the elephant (subconscious cognition) and the rider (conscious cognition) work together to sort through information, form beliefs, decide, and act. The process is imperfect and leads to distortions and biases. We also discussed how we form individual worldviews based on life experience, genetics, and our eternal spirit. Last, we explored how we filter and sort information, sometimes with various forms of cognitive bias preventing us from seeing things clearly and as they really are. This chapter explains the hidden traps on our journeys: ways that people and organizations manipulate us to achieve their own purposes, even if they are harmful to us and society.

The Michael Scott Story

In the "Dunder Mifflin Infinity" episode of the popular television show *The Office*, Michael Scott, the regional manager of a paper company,

---

1. Ardeth G. Kapp, "Young Women Striving Together."
2. Russell M. Nelson, "Peacemakers Needed."
3. Mary Ann Baker, "Master, the Tempest is Raging," 105.

is driving to a country club with his assistant Dwight Schrute to win back lost customers. Michael puts the address in his GPS, which he likes to use because, as he says, it has a soothing voice. As they travel, the GPS tells him to turn right, which Michael insists on doing even though Dwight warns it was referring to the next road and not the boat ramp immediately to their right with the lake clearly in view. Michael, being a slave to the GPS, instead yells to Dwight, "The machine knows!" and drives his car right into the lake. With water pouring into the car, the GPS ironically says, "Make a U-turn if possible."

Just as Michael uncritically followed the GPS to disastrous (and hilarious) results, we often end up following our preconceived models because of their soothing voices or because they had been reliable in the past. Even when our rider sees the proverbial lake, our elephant dives right in. My elephant, my Michael Scott, sometimes barrels ahead into contention even though my rider, my Dwight Schrute, knows it will not end well. Quickly, I find myself in a contentious situation, unable to make a mental U-turn.

Subconscious Cognition is Well Studied

Researchers have dedicated their entire careers to comprehending subconscious cognition—how we shape our worldviews and make decisions influenced by emotions, biases, and moral values. This research, when applied positively, contributes to enhancing our lives. For instance, clinicians utilize insights into subconscious processes to assist diabetics in managing insulin levels, and educators tap into subconscious cues to foster a child's interests and pave the way for lifelong learning. These helpful messages, operating on both conscious and subconscious levels, aim to guide us toward healthier and more informed choices.

While some messaging harnesses subconscious cognition to our benefit, others leverage it to manipulate our actions for their gain. Advertisers skillfully employ words, sounds, and images to evoke emotions like happiness, fear of missing out, or a sense of belonging—all to entice us into purchasing products and services. Market researchers refine these messages through focus groups to alter our beliefs, actions, and purchasing behaviors. While many messages are innocuous or even beneficial, some are so potent that they lead to financial, relationship, or health complications.

Unprincipled individuals and organizations, who "in consequence of evils and designs which do and will exist in the hearts of conspiring men" (D&C 89:4), exploit our cognitive vulnerabilities with meticulously crafted messages. These "bad actors" employ targeted strategies to perpetrate scams and establish control. Whether it involves stealing our money or luring us with unsafe and addictive products, they disregard the harm inflicted on us for their gain.

Reflect

- Do you ever feel forces acting on you to stir up contention or exploit your beliefs, needs, or desires?

- Remember when you bought something that you regret. Perhaps you now realize you were subconsciously manipulated by the seller. What was the manipulative appeal?

In the past couple of decades, as mass media (and our consumption of it) has transitioned from print and broadcast to websites, apps, and streaming services, advertising has also significantly changed from a broader shotgun approach to more targeted marketing. Rather than placing ads in a newspaper or during a television program to reach a general demographic, advertisers are now able to tailor advertising for each individual visitor of a website or user of an app. This is done through data pulled from our web browsing activity, app usage, phone location, and other personal information to make sure that the ads they are spending money on are appearing before the eyes of those most likely to purchase their products and services, and not spent on those who are unlikely to be interested. So now you and I could be reading the exact same article on a news site, but because of our different web searches, past purchases, and social media activity we may see completely different ads on the web page.

Websites, streaming services, and social media companies all depend on the effectiveness of their plans to draw a large audience and then sell data about their audience to those who want to advertise to very specific demographics. This is why you don't pay to use Facebook, YouTube, or TikTok. Instead of charging for services, these businesses profit from using their proprietary algorithms to both promote content they know will keep people's attention and then use that attention to sell advertising. Of course, this has been happening ever since advertising first began appearing in newspapers centuries ago, but in today's online world, it is more exacting and aggressive. A deeper look at social media, and the network Facebook in particular, is a useful example to show how it works.

Social Media Algorithms

Facebook is one of the largest social media networks in the world. It is a free online community where we can connect with clients, businesses, service providers, high school classmates, ward members, mission companions, and people who know us in other settings. We can post our family pictures, our recent vacation, a spiritual thought, an upcoming event, and our thoughts on politics and life. We don't pay anything to use the site since Facebook makes its money by selling advertising to organizations that want to reach us. It's an enormous business; in 2021 Facebook generated $115 billion in revenue from its advertising.[4] They did this by utilizing software and data-based algorithms that decide the content we see, aiming to keep us on their service as much as possible and to deliver ads that align with our interests or are likely to influence us. You can bet they spend millions, maybe billions, of dollars on psychologists, advertising experts, and software designers whose jobs, bonuses, and stock options depend on their effectiveness in getting more people to spend more time on their platform so that they see more ads.

According to the social media consulting company Hootsuite,

> The Facebook algorithm determines which posts people see every time they check their Facebook feed, and in what order those posts show up. Essentially, the Facebook algorithm evaluates every post. It scores posts and then arranges them in descending, non-chronological order of interest for each individual user. . . . We don't know all the details of how the Facebook algorithm decides what to show people (and what not to show people). But we do know . . . one of its goals is to keep people on the platform, so that they see more ads.[5]

Facebook knows our age, gender, religion, marital status, relative income, social communities, where we live, and where we travel—and they use this to not just sell ads but to keep us engaged as much as possible. They understand the elephant and its subconscious thinking and use controversial and divisive issues to attract our attention. Karen Hao, senior artificial intelligence editor at MIT Technology Review, writes, "Just as algorithms [can] be trained to predict who would click what ad, they [can] also be trained to predict who would like or share what post, and then give those posts more prominence.

---

4. Statista Research Department, "Advertising Revenues Generated by Facebook Worldwide from 2017 to 2026."

5. Christina Newberry, "How the Facebook Algorithm Works in 2023 and How to Make it Work for You."

If the model determined a person really liked dogs, for instance, friends' posts about dogs would appear higher up on that user's news feed."[6]

Initially this seems great. After all, who doesn't want to see more of what they want to see? (I'm a dog lover and more posts about dogs seems wonderful.) However, as Hao highlights, there are also some negative and harmful aspects of these algorithms. She says, "The researcher's team . . . found that users with a tendency to post or engage with melancholy content—a possible sign of depression—could easily spiral into consuming increasingly negative material that risked further worsening their mental health."[7] The algorithms do not care whether content is good for us; they are simply programmed to maximize how much content we see and how much time we spend consuming it. Facebook (and its parent company Meta) knows this. A leaked internal presentation warned that Facebook use leads to contention. The anonymous presentation states, "Our algorithms exploit the human brain's attraction to divisiveness. If left unchecked, it would lead users to more and more divisive content to gain user attention & increase time on the platform."[8]

Facebook is not alone in this. Virtually all social media and online advertising companies, including Google, YouTube, TikTok, LinkedIn, Instagram, and Twitter (now X), all have similar algorithms for these same purposes. Hao says of YouTube:

> Because the algorithm is optimized for getting people to engage with videos, it tends to offer choices that reinforce what someone already likes or believes, which can create an addictive experience that shuts out other views. This also often rewards the most extreme and controversial videos, which studies have shown can quickly push people into deep rabbit holes of content [back to the confirmation bias idea—we like what reinforces our existing views] and lead to political radicalization.[9]

We should worry about how social media impacts our children. YouTube is the number one social media platform for Americans between thirteen and seventeen years old. Pew Research says that 95% of this age group uses YouTube, with 19% using it "almost constantly" and 41% using

6. Karen Hao, "The Facebook Whistleblower Says Its Algorithms Are Dangerous. Here's Why."

7. Hao, "The Facebook Whistleblower."

8. Jeff Horwitz and Deepa Seetharaman, "Facebook Executives Shut Down Efforts to Make the Site Less Divisive."

9. Karen Hao, "YouTube Is Experimenting with Ways to Make Its Algorithm Even More Addictive."

it "several times a day."[10] With very little regulation, YouTube algorithms can serve up extreme and controversial videos affecting our youth's worldviews and their perception of what is normal. TikTok has similar usage and might be even worse. According to internet researcher Guillaume Chaslot,

> The TikTok algorithm is more powerful than those used by other social media platforms because it identifies the user's vulnerabilities and exploits them. Within 45 minutes of usage, TikTok is able to determine the user's age, gender, sexual orientation, hobbies, interest, and, yes, even their vulnerabilities. . . . TikTok's secret sauce is mesmerizing and addictive.[11]

These algorithms are like hungry predators, tracking us and looking for their next meal. They subconsciously encourage us to purchase consumer products we can't afford and don't need, push those with melancholic dispositions toward depression, encourage unrealistic body images and eating disorders, and edge people toward political extremism and conspiracy theories.

Try

- Next time you are on social media, ask yourself why the platform shows you what it does.
- While reading, watching, or listening to news media, see if you can identity their algorithm to attract and retain their audiences.
- Do you know any bad actors that advance their causes through lies, to the detriment of society?

Political Messaging

Some political messages are designed to create contentiousness, and they are so powerful and effective that their effects permeate our lives. Such messaging is a powerful force, like gravity drawing everything into a black hole in space, and we feel it at school, in our community, at work, in our families, and even at church. Because these messages are powerful, we are at risk of assimilating the culture of partisan politics into our lives.

Political issues are important, and we are right to focus on them. Governments define the rules for society, touching almost every aspect of our society. They determine communal issues such as economic and social

---

10. Emily A. Vogels, Risa Gelles-Watnick, and Navid Massara, "Teens, Social Media and Technology 2022."

11. Andrew J. Masigan, "TikTok's 'Secret Sauce': Numbers Don't Lie."

policy as well as international relationships. They may also protect us, including our religious and civil rights and our right to hold and express different opinions. We naturally want to elect leaders and implement laws and policies that we think are best for our community and country.

But politics is also a business. In 2020, total spending on national elections for US President, Senate, and House races totaled $14.4 billion.[12] This doesn't count all the state and local elections; this is only donations to national political races. Political media like Fox News, CNN, and MSNBC are also billion-dollar industries, and a large share of what they spend is on political programming. Other industries depend on government policy to make a living, including pharmaceuticals, airlines, and small businesses. Tax policy, immigration, roads and bridges, regulation, and inflation all affect these businesses, so they have reason to be interested in election outcomes. Trillions of dollars are at stake. Just like Facebook and other social media companies, individuals and organizations that are seriously involved in political issues design messages and approaches to create loyalty with voters, get their votes, receive donations, and buy their political products and services.[13]

One such approach is identity politics, in which a political group builds cohesiveness by targeting out-groups through vilification. Identity politics has different dimensions, but it starts with in-group bias, where the algorithm, in this case political programming and messaging, uses our favorable bias for our in-group and our unfavorable bias for our out-groups. It goes beyond tribalism, where we develop loyalty to our political group. Identity politics seeks to destroy any sympathy for other political groups, and today it is being used with greater frequency and more success. It does this by first identifying an issue that is strongly and emotionally held by likely voters, and then creating fear by calling the opposition names and perhaps playing fast and loose with the facts. This is all done to ensure that we view the other group as a villain and as our enemy. The purpose isn't to change one's mind about an issue; it is to instead strengthen loyalty to one group by increasing dislike and even hatred of those portrayed as the opposition. They try to blow up our connections. Sadly, it works.

12. Karl Evers-Hillstrom, "Most Expensive Ever: 2020 Election Cost $14.4 Billion."

13. Such political products and services include consultants, data vendors, marketing lists, media production companies, marketing companies, media subscriptions, hats, yard signs, etc.

Author Ezra Klein summarizes this well: "The increasing levels of anger and fear in the electorate are, from the political system's standpoint, a feature, not a bug. Pew [Research] finds that the angrier and more afraid you are, the likelier you are to actually donate or volunteer."[14] With finite money, politicians know they are able to make us despise others by making their actions seem outrageous and dangerous. Getting you to hate the other party creates more votes for the candidate than trying to convince people that their candidates' positions are best. They are preaching to their own choirs. Klein continues, "The lesson is known by politicians the world over. You don't just need support. You need anger. That's why fund-raising emails often border on the apocalyptic."[15] All sides do it to some extent, and the data shows it works just as they intend.

Contempt is powerful rhetorical messaging that some hyper-partisan news outlets, advocacy groups, and politicians use to stoke anger and outgrouping. In the 2016 presidential election, Hillary Clinton called conservative supporters of Donald Trump "deplorables" and referred to states in the American interior that wouldn't vote for her as "fly over states." Donald Trump referred to supporters of Hillary Clinton as people who "hate America" and are "liberal elites." It's not just them; many advocacy groups, both liberal and conservative, use contemptuous language in fundraising and cause-based work. According to community activist Erica Etelson, "contempt is a first step on the path to dehumanizing the other tribe. If the 'contemptible other' is worthless, then I can safely disregard their hopes and fears. As the distance between us grows, I might become so indifferent as to ignore their suffering or even go to war against them."[16] When we have contempt for our neighbor, it is almost impossible to love them as we love ourselves.

In a 2011 study, a team of political scientists in Nebraska highlight this tactic:

> Potentially more destructive, [this] type of political rhetoric has become more commonplace, what we call political vilification. Partisan disagreements are increasingly steeped in rhetoric that depicts the opposition as the enemy, an enemy that is evil and a threat to the United States and to its

---

14. Ezra Klein, "The Single Most Important Fact About American Politics."
15. Ezra Klein, *Why We're Polarized*, 63.
16. Erica Etelson, *Beyond Contempt: How Liberals Can Communicate Across the Great Divide*, 41.

people. Vilification has become a preferred mode of political rhetoric and its effects are not benign.[17]

Since then it has almost become the norm.

Politicians aren't the only ones who do this. A host of media companies thrive on group-based algorithms. Cable news shows—pick your flavor—all use these algorithms to get their viewers (who likely share similar views) to feel fear or outrage towards their opponents. They use labels like extreme, wacko, radical, fascist, nutjob, and troll to evoke emotions in their in-group, to create more extreme divisions and clearer enemies. Because billions of dollars of revenue are at stake, they do it well, often disregarding accuracy and truth. This messaging isn't news per se; it's just businesses trying to make money by using our subconscious bias to increase their ratings and viewership.

These approaches, whether delivered through social media or through political messaging, are like viruses that unnoticeably infect our thinking. Sadly, there isn't a simple way to inoculate ourselves against such destructive political messaging. They infect through the "us versus them" mentality, harming us both individually and collectively. Even if we don't take part directly, we unknowingly internalize these messages and subconsciously build them into our cognitive models. I'm sure they affect our children even more.

Reflect

- As you read or watch news or political opinions, try and identify the words they use to describe those with opposing views. What emotions are the media trying to cause you to feel?

Negative Conflict's Effects

This polarization doesn't just involve which candidates we like and which policies we pursue; it also affects our acceptance of violence and uncivil behavior. According to a 2019 study, almost all of us agree that this is a problem: "The vast majority—93%—identify incivility as a problem, with most classifying it as a 'major' problem (68%). This disturbing rate has changed little since 2010."[18] The problem doesn't solely lie with group

---

17. Michael W. Wagner, Dona-Gene Mitchell, and Elizabeth Theiss-Morse, "The Consequence of Political Vilification."

18. "Civility in America 2019: Solutions for Tomorrow," Weber Shandwick, 2.

and identity-based messaging but increasingly with the way conflict is overtly used to persuade.

A 2022 study found an increase in incivility by politicians on social media: "Applying a validated artificial intelligence classifier to all 1.3 million tweets made by members of Congress since 2009, we observe a 23% increase in incivility over a decade on Twitter." Why do they do it? Because it works. The study continues: "Uncivil tweets tended to receive more approval and attention, publicly indexed by large quantities of 'likes' and 'retweets' on the platform. Mediational and longitudinal analyses show that the greater this feedback for uncivil tweets, the more uncivil tweets were thereafter."[19]

Content that goes viral can be surprising and packed with positive emotions—like the sixteen-second YouTube video of a kitten getting tickled while lying on her back and all four of her paws going straight up. It puts a smile on my face every time. At the time I write this, it has been viewed over 79 million times.[20] The other way to go viral is to make people angry, disgusted, or any other strong negative emotion. These algorithms work and are often used in politics. They rub off on us, normalizing incivility and conflict.

Immunity from Subconscious Manipulation

The Book of Mormon prophet Lehi says we are "free according to the flesh . . . to act for [our] selves and not be acted upon" (2 Ne. 2:26–27).[21] God gave us the ability to act for ourselves (2 Ne. 2:16).[22] We don't have to fall for these subconscious enticements; instead, we can make reasoned,

---

19. Jeremy Frimer, et al., "Incivility is Rising among American Politicians on Twitter."

20. rozzzafly, "Surprised Kitty (Original)."

21. Lehi didn't say we will ever be free from the effects of bias or physical brain limitations. He did say that no matter what, we can choose eternal life. The limitations of mortality don't take away the choice and agency we have about our eternal welfare.

22. Just as we learn how to recognize the voices of the adversary taking us away from spiritual truths, we can learn to recognize the effects of man-made manipulations designed for their purposes. The warning given as a preface to the Word of Wisdom is equally applicable here: "Behold, verily, thus saith the Lord unto you: In consequence of evils and design which do and will exist in the hearts of conspiring men in the last days, I have warned you, and forewarn you" (D&C 89:4).

conscious choices that move us toward a better world (Ether 12:4).[23] We can teach our subconscious minds (our elephants) and lay aside those things which easily beset us and keep us from fully loving our neighbors (Alma 7:15).[24]

Being free from these negative designs is simple in principle but difficult in practice. Most approaches make powerful but fragile appeals to our subconscious; they lose their power when we consciously examine them. We can expose them by asking ourselves, "What is the subconscious message that they are using to manipulate my bias, subconscious, or cognitive weakness, in order to encourage me to act or feel the way they want?" When we become aware of what they are trying to do to us subconsciously, our conscious rider sees more clearly and can take control of our response.

Here are a few questions to ask yourself that reveal underlying subconscious messaging:

- What is the message's design? That is, what does the message want me to do or feel?

- What is the message trying to get me to do?

- What emotion is the message attempting to create? Is it a negative emotion such as fear, outrage, disgust, or anger?

- How does the message use images, sounds, fonts, and rhetoric to create these emotions?

---

23. Political programming teaches us to be pessimistic about the direction of the world, feeling we live in the worst time ever, with the influences of Satan more pronounced. In reality, we live in the safest, freest, and most opportunity-filled time. Regardless, an essential element of discipleship includes hope in the future. Think of all the times faith, hope, and charity are paired in the scriptures. The middle virtue—hope—is the easiest to overlook. This includes pressing forward in the decisions in our lives and working for a better world, with confidence that eternally, God prevails. Elder Jeffrey R. Holland says, "May we press forward with love in our hearts, walking in the 'brightness of hope' that lights the path of holy anticipation . . . We have every reason to hope for blessings even greater than those we have already received because this is the work of Almighty God." Jeffrey R. Holland, "A Perfect Brightness of Hope."

24. Nephi lamented his tendency to make the same mistakes. He said, "O wretched man that I am! Yea, my heart sorroweth because of my flesh; my soul grieveth because of mine iniquities. I am encompassed about, because of the temptations and the sins which do so easily beset me" (2 Ne. 4:17–18).

- Is the message designed to divide by creating a special, enlightened in-group and an ignorant, villainous out-group?

- When I use social media, what messages are the algorithms showing me? Why?

Chapter 9 includes an exercise, "Evaluate Your Media," that we can do on our own or with another to recognize these subconscious messages and avoid being manipulated. If we consciously examine messages from these actors, our minds will create a subconscious model that will help us see their manipulation and be less susceptible.

With work, we can overcome the natural man and receive blessings by avoiding contention and negativity. With our hearts focused on Zion and its unity, we can set aside contention and division. Seeing others with respect and love will heal our divides.

Book Group Questions

- Which form of contentious messaging do you think is most harmful in society?

- Which manipulative messaging do you think is targeted at you?

- What ways have you used to become immune to destructive subconscious manipulation?

CHAPTER 5

In the World but Not of the World

We need a more peaceful world, growing out of more peaceful families and neighborhoods and communities. To secure and cultivate such peace, 'we must love others, even our enemies as well as our friends.' . . . We need to be kinder, more gentle, more forgiving, and slower to anger. We need to love one another with the pure love of Christ.
—President Howard W. Hunter[1]

Even knowing about all these powers trying to divide us, we need not be discouraged. Yes, today is unique, but mortality has always been full of forces that divide and draw us away from peacemaking. It may be tempting to withdraw from the world, to isolate and await a promised deliverance, but the pathway of discipleship is within the world. We can't love our neighbors if we have none, or if they all look and believe like us. Nor can we "go . . . into all the world and preach the gospel to every creature" if we don't step out our front doors and cross the bridges before us (Mark 16:15). For now, the world is our place of discipleship.

This chapter explains how the gospel of Jesus Christ motivates and supports us as we do God's work, even in a fallen world. These practices not only help us overcome both our biases and the negative influences drawing us into contention, but they also assist us in becoming positive influences in the world. Imagine the impact that millions of Latter-day Saints could have if we were united in peacemaking.

Go Ye into All the World

In the Sermon on the Mount, Jesus taught his followers, "Ye are the light of the world. A city that is set on an hill cannot be hid. Neither do men light a candle, and put it under a bushel, but on a candlestick; and it giveth light unto all that are in the house. Let your light so shine before men, that they may see your good works, and glorify your Father which is in heaven" (Matt. 5:14–16). We cannot be such a light if we strive to entirely separate or isolate ourselves from the rest of the world. Instead, we are repeatedly called to "lift the hands that hang down" (D&C 81:5) and "to be . . . anxiously engaged in a good cause, and do many things of our

---

1. Howard W. Hunter, "A More Excellent Way."

own free will, and bring to pass much righteousness" (D&C 58:27–28). Our problems do not come from being in the world, but from how we engage others from within it. As President Thomas S. Monson teaches us, "Be good citizens of the nations in which we live and good neighbors in our communities, reaching out to those of other faiths, as well as to our own. . . . Be men and women of honesty and integrity in everything we do."[2]

We are most capable of being a light of the world when we have the skills to consider and discuss important issues. Central to these skills is the gospel of Jesus Christ. In a devotional to seminary and institute instructors, Elder Dieter F. Uchtdorf taught, "As you accept the responsibility to seek truth with an open mind and a humble heart, you will become more tolerant of others, more open to listen, more prepared to understand, more inclined to build up instead of tearing down, and more willing to go where the Lord wants you to go."[3] Humility, tolerance, openness, willingness to listen, and the desire to build rather than destroy are the principles of the gospel on which we must ground our engagement in the world.

Consider

- What do you lose when you retreat from discussions about important issues?
- If people like you retreat, what does society lose? Whose voices remain?

Preach the Gospel of Love

At the April 2023 general conference, President Russell M. Nelson issued a call to peacemaking: "Brothers and sisters, the gospel of Jesus Christ has never been needed more than it is today. Contention violates everything the Savior stood for and taught. I love the Lord Jesus Christ and testify that His gospel is the only enduring solution for peace. His gospel is a gospel of peace."[4] As disciples, we invite people to come unto Christ through his gospel message of peace and to join with us on the path of discipleship. Sharing the gospel does not only involve name tags, handing out Book of Mormons, and explicitly sharing our testimonies as we do in Church meetings. We also testify of Jesus through our peacemaking and how we treat and speak with others. As Elder Gary E. Stevenson teaches, "Whenever we

---

2. Thomas S. Monson, "Until We Meet Again."
3. Dieter F. Uchtdorf, "What Is Truth?"
4. Russell M. Nelson, "Peacemakers Needed."

show Christlike love toward our neighbor, we preach the gospel—even if we do not voice a single word. Love for others is the eloquent expression of the second great commandment to love our neighbor."[5]

When we are disciples of Jesus Christ, we put away childish things and dark, earthly glasses so we can see and act clearly and more fully live the two great commandments, to love God and to love our neighbors. President Nelson explains that love in its purest form—charity—is at the center of healing today's divides. He says,

> Charity is the antidote to contention. Charity is the spiritual gift that helps us cast off the natural man, who is selfish, defensive, prideful, and jealous. Charity is the principal characteristic of a true follower of Jesus Christ. Charity defines a peacemaker. . . . One of the best ways we can honor the Savior is to become a peacemaker.[6]

Maintain Self-care and Balance

We are not required to always be the active peacemaker in every difficult and contentious situation. As scripture counsels us, "And see that all these things are done in wisdom and order; for it is not requisite that a man should run faster than he has strength" (Mosiah 4:27). At times we may feel that we must remain silent, or that sometimes silence is the most immediate path to peace—whether it be for the particular situation or because we simply do not have the capacity or energy to have difficult a conversation. When silence, space, or time is needed, it is perfectly okay to stand back, but not because we cease to care or believe it is pointless.

The Ultimate In-group: All Are Children of God

Out-grouping distorts our vision and thinking. It fuels our fears and outrage, diverting us from the love of God and neighbor. Jesus taught a better way. He said, "Love your enemies, bless them that curse you, do good to them that hate you, and pray for them which despitefully use you, and persecute you" (Matt. 5:44). The original Greek translated here as "enemies" is ἐχθρούς (echthrous), which is an adjective and refers to hatred. Another reading would be "love those that hate us." This is a revolutionary teaching and one we cannot exemplify from under a bushel, as it does not involve a casual sentiment but an active, deep, and profound

5. Gary E. Stevenson, "Love, Share, Invite."
6. Nelson, "Peacemakers Needed."

love. According to President Gordon B. Hinckley, "Most of us have not reached that stage of compassion and love and forgiveness. It requires a self-discipline almost greater than we are capable of."[7] To this, President Dallin H. Oaks adds, "It is possible, if we ask, for He also taught, 'Ask, and it shall be given you; seek, and ye shall find.'"[8] When we can actually find it within us to love those who despise us, we find growth and create goodness. But, it's a hard saying, and many turn away (John 6:60).

The less we describe people who think or behave differently as enemies, the better. Even if they have left the Church, have different political beliefs, or act in ways we find immoral, each person still has good qualities as well as weaknesses. Thinking of them instead as brothers and sisters pulls them into our in-group and causes our brains to use a different region than what we use when thinking about the out-group. It literally changes the way we think about them. This is also true for the politicians, celebrities, and personalities that dominate the headlines.

Potential Conflicts Between Worldviews and Morality

There is unequivocal right and wrong. Murder, rape, slavery, and child abuse are all evil. We pass laws against these practices, only disagreeing about how to punish perpetrators. We believe we should protect the innocent, take care of the disadvantaged, and create a fair society with opportunity for all, but we also have different opinions and beliefs about how to go about it. Our sincere and well-thought-out beliefs thus lead us to different preferred policies to address these problems.

Even with common spiritual beliefs, we may end up with different political beliefs. Latter-day Saints holding the same values may differ politically on the level of which of those values should be imposed on others. For example, despite clear statements by Church leaders that abortion is sin, in a February 2023 poll, 32% of Latter-day Saints said that abortion should be legal in all or most cases, while 68% said that it should be illegal in all or most cases.[9] Likewise, despite the Church's position that marriage should only be between a man and a woman, Latter-day Saints are also divided on their support of legalized same sex marriage, with 46% sup-

---

7. Gordon B. Hinckley, "The Healing Power of Christ."

8. Dallin H. Oaks, "Love Your Enemies."

9. PRRI Staff, "Abortion Attitudes in a Post-Roe World: Findings From the 50-State 2022 American Values Atlas."

porting and 54% opposing.[10] Those Latter-day Saints who responded may fully sustain Church positions for how members should act but differ in whether their beliefs should govern the lives of others.

In some of today's most divisive issues, our individual moral and spiritual beliefs lead us to different political beliefs and policy preferences. Using abortion as an example, the Southern Baptist Convention states that life and ensoulment (when the spirit enters the body) occurs at conception.[11] Thus, most Southern Baptists want to pass laws to prohibit abortion, with few if any exceptions. They believe they need to protect life, even the single cell at conception, because it has a human soul.

By contrast, the National Council of Jewish Women, representing Reform Jews, states that the fetus is part of the mother until birth. Just as Adam did not become a living soul until God breathed spirit into him (Gen. 2:7), for these Jews it is not until the newborn baby takes its first breath that there is a new and distinguished living soul.[12] Thus, most Reform Jews want to leave abortion decisions to the mother.

What would a conversation about abortion between a Southern Baptist man and a Reform Jewish woman look like? Perhaps they would ask about the underlying reasons for their beliefs on abortion. They could explore their moral values, and they might agree that they both value life and a women's ability to choose. They might not find common ground about laws regulating abortion, but they could learn that the other's beliefs come from their sincere moral and religious values. Neither could prove when the soul enters the body, but they could agree about the soul's divinity and respect that the other person has deep religious and spiritual beliefs. Their beliefs about abortion would likely be unreconcilable, but their understanding and respect for the other person could be strengthened as they see each other as well-intentioned, faithful people making moral decisions from their respective worldviews.

On the other hand, their conversation could also end up contentious, with one asking why they support killing babies and the other denouncing patriarchy and asking why legislatures dominated by men want to take away a woman's choices about her body. They would leave distrust-

---

10. "American's Support for Key LGBTQ Rights Continues to Tick Upwards, Findings from the 2021 American Values Atlas," PRRI.

11. Scott F. Gilbert, Anna L. Tyler, and Emily Zackin, *Bioethics and the New Embryology: Springboard for Debate*, 39.

12. "Judaism and Abortion," National Council of Jewish Woman.

ful, angry, feeling disrespected, and with their sincere religious and moral values misunderstood.

Similar results often come from discussions between Latter-day Saints who disagree on policies around abortion law and same-sex marriage. Despite coming from similar religious beliefs, most of these discussions end in some kind of name-calling and alienation. For some, their alienation is so complete that they feel their personal beliefs require them to leave the Church. Others label them as wayward or apostates, saying "Good riddance" when they see them slam the door on their way out. On the other hand, in those few conversations where people have respected the others' moral values and sought to understand their reasoning, participants leave with feelings of trust and respect, even if they still disagree.

Even as we sustain prophets and believe in the doctrines of the Church, our worldviews and moral values lead us to different political policies. While we all believe that slavery and racism are wrong, we have mixed morally based views on other issues such as immigration, education, and wealth inequality, each having a significant moral component. As the Prophet Joseph Smith once said, "I teach them [Latter-day Saints] correct principles, and they govern themselves." Every member incorporates the principles of the gospel into their unique worldview as we each strive to do what we think is right.

Our individual worldviews are influenced by the events and cultures in which we grow up. The worldviews of both younger and older Latter-day Saints were formed in different times, often leading to different religious and political perspectives. For example, 59% of American Latter-day Saint millennials (born 1980–1998) agree with this statement: "The fact that women do not hold the priesthood sometimes bothers me," while only 24% of American Latter-day Saint boomer and silent generations (born 1928–1964) agree.[13] In the 2020 presidential election, surveys estimate that only 42% of Latter-day Saints under 40 voted Republican, while 80% of those 40 and older voted Republican.[14] Different generations see the world differently, even within the Church.

Gender also affects our worldviews, with women and men often having different political priorities. That's not surprising, since women and men experience the world differently and have different preferences. According

---

13. Jana Riess, *The Next Mormons: How Millennials Are Changing the LDS Church*, 98.

14. Jana Riess, "Younger US Mormons Voted for Biden, but Trump Performed Well Overall."

to the Center for American Women and Politics, "women tend to be more supportive of gun control, reproductive rights, welfare, and equal rights policies than men. They tend to be less supportive of the death penalty, defense spending, and military intervention. Recent polls found that, compared with men, women are slightly more optimistic and/or satisfied with the direction in which the country is going."[15] Each gender experiences life differently and views things the other does not. Likewise, transgender and non-binary individuals have unique and important perspectives and life experiences. We need to understand others' worldviews and try to understand things that we haven't experienced. We all have blind spots about big issues, and we can benefit from understanding what others see that we do not.

Reflect
• Why do you think there are such dramatic differences in political preference in the age groups mentioned above? • What can you learn from these other age groups? • What can you learn from other genders?

Conflicts on Moral Issues

How should we respond to others' differing beliefs on what we see as important moral issues? Later chapters provide specific tools and approaches for these conversations, but here is a quick summary of how to approach these important and essential discussions:

- Start with respecting and dignifying the other person and their beliefs. Assume that they come from sincere moral values and their own rational worldview. Try to understand not only what they believe, but the values and experiences that help form their belief. Then see if you can repeat back to someone their moral reasoning to make sure you understand it. When we understand why they believe something, it's easier to respect their point of view and find common ground.

- Be open and consider their viewpoint. Remember our tendency toward competency and contact bias, in which we think we have fully considered something when we haven't. If you are open, you will likely learn something since their worldview is different and likely involves different points than what you have fully considered.

---

15. Center for American Women and Politics, "Gender Gap Public Opinion."

- Similarly, your perspectives, values, and worldviews can help others see things they couldn't otherwise. While there are times to be quiet, don't retreat. Remember Alma's counsel to his son Shiblon: "Use boldness, but not overbearance; . . . bridle all your passions, that ye may be filled with love" (Alma 38:12).

Historically, moral values have generally emerged from religion, but as society changes, many who disaffiliate from organized religion may instead root their values in their deep personal convictions. Accommodating diverse moral and spiritual beliefs can be difficult and complicated. Some non-religious people report discrimination at school and in the workplace, including physical assault from religious people and rejection by family and friends.[16] Likewise, those of faith may find their beliefs mocked or treated with similar disrespect or ill treatment. Should we afford people with non-religious moral beliefs the same standing as those who belong to a specific religion? Should we grant someone a religious exemption for COVID-19 vaccination if it violates their personal beliefs, even if they don't belong to a specific faith? Should a non-religious baker be able to refuse service to a member of an offensive, intolerant religious group like the Westboro Baptist Church[17] (known for their verbally abusive picket lines at military funerals and similar tactics)? It's complex, living in a society with different beliefs and worldviews.[18]

Can godly people, including believing Latter-day Saints, have different worldviews, or is there simply right and wrong? The answer is yes. We each have different beliefs about the world and different priorities about the changes we want to see. Each view is legitimate and understandable because it comes from the unique ways in which we experience the world.

Spiritual Practices for Dealing with Difference

Here are four spiritual skills that are helpful in healing our divides. Find others by pondering and praying about which spiritual principles can help you be a better peacemaker.

---

16. S. Frazer, A. El-Shafei, and A. M. Gill, *Reality Check: Being Nonreligious in America.*

17. See Robert Lewis, "Westboro Baptist Church."

18. For more information on religious exemptions, see Movement Advancement Project, "Talking about Religious Exemption Laws."

Weed Out the Bitter Root

The first practice involves self-reflection, starting with an internal examination. In his epistle to the Hebrews, Paul warns, "Let no root of bitterness spring up and trouble you, lest many be defiled by it" (Heb. 12:15, Revised Geneva Translation). Paul recognized that most people have a dark, angry, or fearful side to their nature. If left unchecked, this bitterness can grow and harm those around us, leading to animosity and contention.

We can check this bitterness by recalling instances where we have felt contempt and contention and investigating the root cause of these feelings within ourselves. We may ask ourselves questions such as "Why does this issue make me angry?" or "What am I afraid of?" We may also consider what it is about a particular topic or person that generates such strong emotions. It is possible that we have unresolved issues that make this topic painful, or we may be projecting our pain or fear onto the other person and holding them responsible for it.

The bitter root can have many causes, and by looking inward, we have an opportunity to heal from past wounds and fears that distort our perspective and create contempt towards others. This practice allows us to gain greater self-awareness and to work toward developing a more compassionate and understanding approach toward those with differing viewpoints.

Practice Empathy and Compassion

When Jesus said to love our neighbors, he said, "love your neighbors *as yourself*" (Matt. 22:39; emphasis added). That means we expand our understanding to appreciate who they are, how they think, and what is important to them. Henri Nouwen, a Dutch Catholic priest, described this practice beautifully when he said, "Compassion asks us to go where it hurts, to enter into the places of pain, to share in brokenness, fear, confusion, and anguish. . . . Compassion means full immersion in the condition of being human."[19]

This practice is at the heart of the Atonement of Jesus Christ. According to the prophet Alma, Jesus "will take upon him [our] infirmities, that his bowels may be filled with mercy . . . that he may know according to the flesh how to succor his people according to their infirmities" (Alma

---

19. Donald P. McNeill, Douglas A. Morrison, and Henri J. M. Nouwen, *Compassion: A Reflection on the Christian Life*, 4.

7:12).[20] Jesus knows us completely in a divine way. Similarly, our efforts to understand someone else is a divine work, emulating Christ's atoning mission in our own humble lives.

This is a hard practice that takes time and effort—something we simply cannot spend on everyone who disagrees with us. However, it's worth the effort with close family members or associates with whom we must regularly engage. Real listening gives us greater insight into the issues that divide us. We will learn how they came to believe what they do, and we may find common ground that can pull them into our in-group and remove the out-group bias we would have otherwise. If we can't do that, we can at least ask ourselves, "What in their life might have contributed to their differing opinion?" If time permits, we can ask them what led them to their belief.

Reflect and Try

- Reflect—How does the spiritual practice of empathy impact your everyday view of others?
- Reflect—Have you ever been gifted to see—truly see—someone with whom you disagree?
- Try—Ask curious questions to understand someone else, to better appreciate where they are coming from and why they think as they do.

Be Humble about Our Certainty

Some truths are simple and provable, such as math facts and basic scientific principles. But for many issues, we can't fully understand all the complexities or be certain of our own interpretations.

Even wise men are humble about their certainty. After Moses spoke with the Lord on Mount Sinai and was given a vision of all the creation, he declared, "Now, for this cause I know that man is nothing, which thing I never had supposed" (Moses 1:10).[21] Like Moses, our knowledge of God and His works is limited, and the same goes with our knowledge of today's complex issues. The Book of Mormon prophet Jacob knew this and

---

20. Empathy is part of the Atonement of Jesus Christ. "Because Jesus Christ endured the infinite atoning sacrifice, He *empathizes* perfectly with us. He is always aware of us and our circumstances." Dale G. Renlund, "Infuriating Unfairness"; emphasis added.

21. "Is not Moses' recognition of our complete dependence on God the beginning of true humility?" Marlin K. Jensen, "To Walk Humbly with Thy God."

taught his people, "O the vainness, and the frailties, and the foolishness of men! When they are learned they think they are wise, and they hearken not unto the counsel of God, for they set it aside, supposing they know of themselves, wherefore, their wisdom is foolishness and it profiteth them not. And they shall perish" (2 Ne. 9:28). Shakespeare felt the same. Through the voice of Touchstone in the play *As You Like It*, he says, "The fool doth think he is wise, but the wise man knows himself to be a fool."[22]

We all have more misconceptions and misunderstandings about the complex issues of today than we tend to recognize, and so practicing humility about our certainty involves pausing and considering what we might not know. It includes saying things such as "Let me think about that," "I'm not sure," "I don't know," "You're right, I hadn't thought of that," and even sometimes "I'm wrong; thank you for helping me see." It is always better to be curious, ask questions, and listen to people with different life experiences and expertise. We should always be open to learning more and never be certain we fully understand.

While working and thinking in groups tends to bring us closer to the truth than we can get individually, our groups can still be wrong—they are full of humans after all. Even when we strive to receive divine inspiration, all groups make mistakes. Like personal humility, we can have group humility. When our church, political party, or even the running club to which we belong makes a mistake, we should acknowledge that our group is wrong. As Elder Dieter F. Uchtdorf humbly acknowledges,

> To be perfectly frank, there have been times when members or leaders in the Church have simply made mistakes. There may have been things said or done that were not in harmony with our values, principles, or doctrine. I suppose the Church would be perfect only if it were run by perfect beings. God is perfect, and His doctrine is pure. But He works through us—His imperfect children—and imperfect people make mistakes.[23]

This is a stunning teaching. If our Church, being led by prophets and apostles, can make mistakes, it is clear that our preferred political party, candidate, scientific society, sports team, and alma mater can make a lot of

---

22. William Shakespeare, *As You Like It*, act V, scene I.

23. Dieter F. Uchtdorf, "Come, Join with Us." Elder Holland said something similar: "Except in the case of His only perfect Begotten Son, imperfect people are all God has ever had to work with. That must be terribly frustrating to Him but He deals with it. So should we. And when you see imperfection, remember that the limitation is not in the divinity of the work." Jeffrey R. Holland, "Lord, I Believe."

them. If we cannot see or acknowledge those mistakes, we are simply un-prepared to have peaceful and meaningful discussions and relationships.

Latter-day Saint political scientist Valerie Hudson explains the inher-ent limitations in social structures, including the Church:

> In my research I study micro-levels of decision-making, such as personal-ity, perception, group dynamics, and culture, the fact that these forces are at work in the Church's bureaucracy has not dampened my testimony one whit. What it has done, however, is appropriately lower my expectations of Church institutional behavior. Using my FPA [foreign policy analysis] skills, I am able to see the fallible humans within Church institutions and the dysfunctional group decision-making that sometimes ensues. I honor the doctrine and revelations of the Church even as I recognized that many of the Church's policies and programs seeking to instantiate those doctrines and revelations have been created much like the proverbial sausage. . . . However, because as a fallible mortal I am hoping for mercy from the Lord myself, I feel to forgive, for I have finally learned that this world was *meant* to be a messy, hurtful learning experience and was never meant to be a place run efficiently or justly. But my dearest hope is that there is such a place. [24]

Because of in-group bias, we are less able to see mistakes in those who believe like us. Sometimes we have to look for them, but they are there. When we are able to recognize the mistakes of *our side* in a conversation, it changes the tone and reduces entrenchment and defensiveness. It builds or strengthens our connection with others, establishes a pattern of open thinking, and just might help others own their mistakes as well. That's not why we do it—it's not a transaction—but owning the mistakes in our own beliefs makes it easier for the other side to admit they are wrong as well.

We should also strive to avoid excusing mistakes *on our side* because the *other side* has made errors that are just as bad or even worse. This is called whataboutism—a term that Merriam-Webster recently added to its dictionary as "the act or practice of responding to an accusation of wrongdoing by claiming that an offense committed by another is similar or worse."[25] Wrong is wrong. It's always wrong, and we shouldn't defend it simply because the *other side* has done wrong in a comparable way.

I own a small business that does electronic repair in Washington DC, located in a retail area within walking distance from the US Capitol build-ing. After George Floyd's murder on May 25, 2020, there was rioting and

---

24. Valerie M. Hudson, "The Two-Way Street of Faith and Scholarship: A Political Scientist's Experience"; emphasis in the original.

25. Merriam-Webster.com Dictionary, "Whataboutism."

looting in Washington, including where my store is located. Every night for a week I emptied out my store, including our inventory, equipment, and all customer devices awaiting repair, in case we were looted. Months later, on January 6, 2021, we had to close business for two days because of violence at the nearby US Capitol. Because of our proximity, the FBI visited us and asked us for copies of our video security tapes from January 5 and 6.

No matter who we are and how we identify politically, we should denounce the violence at the US Capitol, the violence following George Floyd's murder, and the few instances of violence during the BLM protests.[26] Some use the violence of one of these events to minimize the violence of the other event. In addition to whataboutism, sometimes we express false equivalency, in which two events with common issues are treated the same. It is a false equivalency when people equate the US Capitol riots and the riots after George Floyd's murder or suggest they are opposite sides of the same coin. While both were acts of violence, they were completely different in motive and intent.[27] Using whataboutism or falsely equating events causes us to gloss over important details and excuse the wrong on *our side*. As the saying goes, "Clean up your own backyard."

Consider and Try
• Consider whether it's okay to be sure of what you know, but leave a little bit of space to change your mind as you learn something. • Try pausing and asking yourself about the limits of your knowledge and how much of the issue you truly understand.

26. BLM protests had few instances of violence. A Harvard study showed that "96.3% of events involved no property damage or police injuries, and in 97.7% of events, no injuries were reported among participants, bystanders or police." See Erica Chenoweth and Jeremy Pressman, "This summer's Black Lives Matter protesters were overwhelmingly peaceful, our research finds."

27. The Associated Press, a news source assessed as non-biased and reliable, reported that "the two events were fundamentally different. One was an intentional, direct attack on a hallowed democratic institution, with the goal of overturning a fair and free election. The other was a coast-to-coast protest movement demanding an end to systemic racism that occasionally, but not frequently, turned violent." See Julie Watson, "Comparison between Capitol siege, BLM protests is denounced."

Listen with Curiosity, Seek to Understand

Listening is intertwined with empathy, understanding, and humility. It honors the dignity of others by letting them know we value them and their perspective, and it opens us up to learning about them and what they think. Through listening, the other person feels heard and valued. As author David Augsburger beautifully says, "Being heard is so close to being loved that for the average person, they are almost indistinguishable."[28] Likewise, Ralph Nichols describes founding The International Listening Association in part because he feels that "the most basic of all human needs is to understand and be understood. The best way to understand people is to listen to them."[29] True listening is an expansion that activates our conscious thinking and opens us up to being willing to change our current models of belief. We become curious, humble, and willing to learn because we are genuinely interested in the other person.

A spiritual practice that can prepare us to be better listeners involves first pausing and trying to silence your mind, and then visualizing the other person as a part of your in-group by finding something in common. Afford them dignity and recognize that they have unique experiences that can teach something valuable. Think of questions to get to know them better. A simple phrase such as "I'd be curious to know. . ." can spark curiosity about the other person—where they come from, what they have experienced, and why they believe this or that. A curious mind almost always leads to becoming a better listener.[30]

As you do this, take note of whether you are talking more or less than the other person. If you think you are talking half the time, it means you are probably talking 75% of the time. If you set a goal to talk 33% or less, then you are likely succeeding in listening to understand someone else. Even if you are naturally a listener, think about questions you can ask that are genuinely curious to better understand what the other person is saying and feeling.

In 2022, the Church released the Institute of Religion course "Answering My Gospel Questions" (REL 280). Among its "microtrainings" to help class participants with specific topics is "Five Ways to Be a Good Listener."[31] They are:

---

28. David W. Augsburger, *Caring Enough to Hear and Be Heard*.

29. Ralph G. Nichols, *Are You Listening*.

30. This is discussed further in chapter 7.

31. "Microtraining 5: How to Be an Active Listener," Answering My Gospel Questions Teacher Material (Religion 280).

- *Give people time.* Be patient and allow people time to think and speak before and after they say something. Don't be afraid of silence.

- *Pay attention.* Really listen to understand and don't make premature conclusions or think ahead about what you are going to say.

- *Clarify.* Ask clarifying questions to show interest in what the person is saying and to make sure you don't misunderstand.

- *Reflect.* Paraphrase or restate what you feel the person is saying. This gives the speaker a chance to feel validated and to clarify as needed.

- *Find common ground.* Agree with the person as much as possible, without misrepresenting your own feelings, to help build unity and reduce any anxiety or defensiveness.

To these great principles, we can add:

- People listen better when the TV is off, when they aren't on their phones, and when there is enough time.

- Listening happens better in person. It can be effective on the phone and online, but it's even better when we see each other and can pay attention to body language and tone of voice. Listening happens worst in texts, emails, and on social media.

- Refrain from rebutting, testifying, and correcting what you think might be wrong. Listening isn't a debate; it's a time to explore what the other person thinks and feels.

- Don't build false equivalency in your experiences. Sometimes we may think that sharing a similar experience will connect us, but it rarely does. While it may be a well-intentioned attempt to show empathy, it changes the subject to ourselves and replaces listening with being listened to. At worst, it may start a game of competitive rivalry, trying to outdo each other to prove who had the hardest experience.

Why does listening feel like love? Listening is ultimately a selfless act. It tells the other person you value them and want to understand them, not because you think you are wiser, but because you care about them. It's a spiritual practice because it is elevating and fits into the pattern of God, who listens to our prayers, no matter how childish and simple they are. He cares. He is eager to hear from us. As we develop and use this skill, we find that we and the other person "both are edified and rejoice together," and contention decreases (D&C 50:22).

> **Try and Reflect**
>
> • Have a conversation with the goal of spending 80% or more of the discussion listening. Try to only ask questions.
>
> • Did you feel more connected? Were you more open to learning?
>
> • What did you give up? Anything?

Anything that builds love and connection comes from spiritual principles, which are rooted in our Savior. As President Nelson testifies, "There is one source to whom we can all turn to either enhance the love we feel for others or mend our hearts when they feel broken—the Savior Jesus Christ."[32] We are called to be peacemakers in a world filled with its differences, incivility, and acrimony. God wants us to do it in love, as we would like to be treated. He commands us to love our neighbors, strangers, and those who hate us.[33] That's everyone.

> **Book Group Questions**
>
> • Which practices are most helpful for you?
>
> • What did you learn from identifying the things *I know that I don't know*, the things that *I think I know*, and the things *I know that I know*?
>
> • How hard is it to be genuinely curious when you are listening?

---

32. Ryan Jensen, "In Valentine's Day message, President Nelson asks for an increase in 'lovingkindness.'"

33. Scriptures are replete with calls to love everyone. Our guide should be to treat all people like ourselves. "Therefore all things whatsoever ye would that men should do to you, do ye even so to them: for this is the law and the prophets" (Matt. 7:12). We should embrace the stranger: "And if a stranger sojourn with thee in your land, ye shall not vex him. But the stranger that dwelleth with you shall be unto you as one born among you, and thou shalt love him as thyself; for ye were strangers in the land of Egypt" (Lev. 19:33–34). We even are commanded to love those who hate us: "But I say to you, Love your enemies and pray for those who persecute you" (Matt. 5:44).

CHAPTER 6

Preparatory Tools

*But I say, if you are even angry with someone, you are subject to judgment!
If you call someone an idiot, you are in danger of being brought before
the court. And if you curse someone, you are in danger of the fires of hell.*
—Matthew 5:22, New Living Translation

*If there are barriers, it is because we ourselves have created them. We
must stop concentrating on our differences and look for what we have in
common; then we can begin to realize our greatest potential and achieve
the greatest good in this world.*
—Sister Bonnie L. Oscarson[1]

When I was a teenager, I spent a summer doing construction work—
more correctly, I was a go-fer (you know, someone who would go fer this,
go fer that). By the end of the summer, I could do rough construction
and dig really nice holes. Besides learning unique ways to swear without
swearing, I learned that with the right tools, the job is easier and the
results are better.

When you build a house, a skilled architect works with you to create
a design and then translates it into blueprints. Then your contractor takes
the blueprints and lays it out on the construction site. They measure exactly where the foundation, walls, and electrical outlets will be so it looks
exactly like what you designed. Before they pound a nail, set a screw, or
cut a board, they make sure they know what and where they are building.

So it is with peacemaking. With a proper foundation we can have
meaningful and productive discussions—even about difficult topics. With
the right tools, we can clarify what we want to get out of any conversation and create the right setting to achieve it. While these tools work for
planned conversations, with practice we can draw on them even when an
ordinary conversation turns unexpectedly heated. The more we use these
skills, the more proficient we will be at using them.

These tools are summarized here and explained later in the chapter.
Practice them until they become natural.

- **Set your goals**—Step back and decide what you want to accomplish
  with the conversation. You may want to build relationships, under-

---

1. Bonnie L. Oscarson, "Sisterhood: Oh, How We Need Each Other."

stand others, find solutions, or change minds. Clarifying what you want and understanding how to go about it is an important part of eliminating contention.

- **Assess potential disagreement**—Many conversations are about what we agree on. Some topics have minor disagreements, while others have such little common ground that they are very difficult. Just knowing the level of potential disagreement helps you know how to handle the discussion.

- **Determine the potential cost**—Having conversations about difficult topics requires time and energy. You may risk alienation, loss of status, and being perceived negatively when others think your position is wrong. Before you begin such conversations, consider what cost you may need to pay. Some topics are so important that you may be willing to pay a high cost to try creating change; conversely, you may realize a topic is not important enough to risk any costs to yourself or your relationships.

- **Create the right setting**—You can't achieve your goals unless you have the right setting. Set it up right, and you will get better results.

- **Find and use reliable information**—Meaningful discussions benefit from having information that is reliable and trustworthy.

- **Emotionally prepare**—Some conversations are difficult and can tax us emotionally. Prepare when you want or need to have these conversations so that you have the right emotional foundation.

These tools will each be explored in detail below, but come back to this summary whenever you need to refresh and check them off before participating in a potentially difficult conversation.

Set Your Conversation Goals

In the midst of a discussion, we may often find ourselves feeling like Alice talking to the Cheshire Cat in *Alice in Wonderland:*

Alice: Would you tell me, please, which way I ought to go from here?

The Cheshire Cat: That depends a good deal on where you want to get to.

Alice: I don't much care where.

The Cheshire Cat: Then it doesn't much matter which way you go.

Alice: . . . So long as I get somewhere.

The Cheshire Cat: Oh, you're sure to do that, if only you walk long enough.[2]

If we don't think about our conversation goals, we may wander and end up somewhere we didn't want to go. We may find ourselves in contentious discussions, and we may possibly alienate our relationships. Before starting, be thoughtful and decide what kind of conversation is intended, as each objective needs different tools and approaches. If the conversation veers off track, pause and reset.

You may have a particular goal for a discussion, but others in the group may not share it. Consider what they may want to achieve and adapt your objectives to something everyone can understand and support. It is almost always better to be open and clear about your conversation goals rather than silently hoping the discussion sticks to them. Ask everyone by saying something like, "We are talking about something that is controversial. What would everyone like to get out of this conversation?" Then state some possible goals described below. With shared expectations, the conversation is less likely to go off the rails.

Some helpful conversation objectives include:[3]

Goal: Build Connection and Relationship

We can seek a conversation to learn about others and find out what they think. These conversations build trust, uncover things in common, and strengthen relationships. The ideas can be difficult, controversial, or mundane; the topic doesn't matter as much as how we talk about them. Good topics include those that are important to the other person because they help us understand their concerns, interests, experience, and how they came to believe what they do. Do not be concerned with whether you share their beliefs; instead, simply care to know where they are coming from. Talk and ask questions, but especially focus on listening with interest and curiosity.

Goal: Learn from Others

Regardless of how much we think we know about a topic, always approach conversations with a desire to learn something. We come as active learners, open to developing or changing our opinions based on others'

---

2. Lewis Carroll, *Alice in Wonderland*, ch. 6.

3. Adapted from Peter Boghossian and James Lindsay, *How to Have Impossible Conversations, A Very Practical Guide*, 10–11.

expertise or life experience. This requires being honest to ourselves about this goal. We can't pretend to be learning from another when our actual goal is simply to change their mind by having *them* listen to *us*. Pause, then reflect on whether we are open to examining our own beliefs before setting this as our goal.

Goal: Change Others' Opinions and Beliefs

Trying to change someone's belief is a legitimate and important conversational objective. As Latter-day Saints, we want to heal the world and make it better. Our prayers aren't just for our individual welfare or for that of our families; we pray for others too, even the entire kingdom of God and beyond. Jesus commanded us to love God, and in the same breath asked us to love and care for our neighbors. As followers of Jesus, we are to be kind and civil; at the same time, we are to be "anxiously engaged in a good cause . . . to bring to pass much righteousness" (D&C 58:27).

There are ethical and unethical ways to try to change others. As Latter-day Saints, we honor agency—the ability of a person to choose their own beliefs—and thus we should invite and persuade rather than coerce and control.[4] Unethical coercion occurs when someone feels they have no choice but to agree or they must face difficult consequences for disagreeing. (It also never works long-term.) Ethical persuasion allows one to disagree and reject others' beliefs without a fear of retribution, punishment, or loss of status by either person. According to David McRaney, persuasion is preferable to coercion because it "lead[s] a person along in

---

4. See D&C 121:41. Those who use the righteous principles outlined in verses 41–43, including kindness, long-suffering, gentleness, and meekness, are promised they will receive power that comes naturally and almost unseen. "And the doctrine of the priesthood shall distil upon thy soul as the dews from heaven. The Holy Ghost shall be thy constant companion, and thy scepter an unchanging scepter of righteousness and truth; and thy dominion shall be an everlasting dominion, and *without compulsory means* it shall flow unto thee forever and ever" (D&C 121:45–46; emphasis added). Note: some use "reproving betimes with sharpness" (D&C 121:43) as license to argue or tell people what they should believe. But reproving means correcting gently, betimes means speedily, and sharpness means clarity, as in a camera in sharp focus. This scripture then reads "gently correcting speedily with clarity." This completely changes the tone. See "Line Upon Line: Doctrine and Covenants 121:41–43," *New Era.*

stages, helping them to better understand their own thinking and how it could align with the message at hand."[5]

Reflect
• Think back to the last conversation in which you wanted to change someone's mind. Did you use anything you now realize might be perceived as coercive? Or do you think they felt safe to disagree? • Did you feel you could disagree without fear of negative consequences? Was it safe for you to disagree?

Goal: Come to Agreement

Here we all share the goal of exploring a topic and coming to a mutual understanding, where all participants are willing to give up old opinions and correct mistaken beliefs if needed. It requires humility, openness, and a willingness to examine the limitations of how we arrived at previously held opinions and beliefs.

For complex and morally based issues, our efforts should center on understanding others' moral values and why they believe they do. Ask questions about their worldviews and what events and values led them to their belief. The discussion proceeds with dignity and respect, under the assumption that other participants have sincere reasons for why they believe what they do. Assume that you have common ground and work to find it. Don't expect to resolve complicated issues in a single conversation; some topics take time and multiple discussions to reflect and consider others' points.

Complimentary Goals

Despite our best efforts and well-intentioned goals, when we try to change others' opinions and beliefs or mutually come to agreement, there is still potential for conflict and contention. No one wants to be told they are wrong. When coming to a discussion with these goals, consider the following before proceeding:

- **Consider religious beliefs.** In testimony meetings, we often hear people say they know certain beliefs are true. We come to these beliefs through spiritual processes as we "test the word of God" by planting the seed to see if it grows, not through rational or scientific pro-

---

5. David McRaney, *How Minds Change: The Surprising Science of Belief, Opinion, and Persuasion*, xviii.

cesses (Alma 32:28–43). People change their religious views based on spiritual experiences, not through logical discussions. Missionaries are taught to not *Bible bash*, as it almost always becomes contentious; instead, they are instructed to invite as the Savior did, so the investigator can explore and determine for themselves and develop their own faith. The Church instructs teachers to follow this pattern: "From the beginning of His ministry, the Savior invited His followers to experience for themselves the truths, power, and love that He offered."[6] We first *build connections and relationships*. Then we can *learn from others* and *find truth*. With those objectives, our conversation partners become more open to accepting invitations.

- **Understand your own certainty about the discussion topic.** Before we set a goal of trying to change someone's mind, we should evaluate our level of certainty about our own belief and recognize that our certainty may vary between different aspects of the same topic. Use a scale of 1 (low) to 10 (high) to measure the certainty of both your position and your proposal on how to best solve it.

  For example, let's say you are almost certain immigration is not a problem. Your certainty may be a 9, but you may only be a 2 when it comes to thinking the best change we could make is to disband or reform ICE (Immigration and Customs Enforcement). Another person may be almost certain (9) that immigration is a problem, but they may be less certain (maybe 3) that building a wall on the southern border is the best solution. Our certainty about something being a problem is always higher than our certainty about how to solve it because pointing to an issue is always easier than knowing how to resolve it.

  As we assess our certainty, we should also assess our competency bias (where we think we are more knowledgeable than we really are), group bias (when we are more likely to believe talking points said by our own group than by others), and how those factors affect our certainty. With immigration, does our certainty come from reading a variety of studies about how immigration affects our country? Or has our opinion been primarily formed by political programing from news media or candidates that seek to emotionally manipulate our subconscious minds for our money or our votes?

---

6. "Invite Diligent Learning," *Teaching in the Savior's Way: For All Who Teach in the Home and in the Church.*

Evaluating our certainty about a belief is an important skill. If we are certain enough, we may try to *persuade others*; if not, it may be better to set a goal to *learn from others* while we continue to ponder thorny issues.

Consider
• What is an issue in which you want to change someone's mind?
• Is there an issue in which someone would want to change your mind?
• How confident are you that you could have those conversations without contention?

Ineffective and Counterproductive Goals

Not all goals are helpful. Some discussions are merely soapboxes, with one person sending a message and telling others what they should think. If we are approaching a conversation with a mindset such as *I really need to tell someone what I think and set them straight*, then pause and consider why we want to do that and what we hope will happen. Telling people what to believe rarely works; instead, it almost always alienates. Some tools are effective in helping change someone's belief, but it almost never happens through one-sided explaining, preaching, or testifying.

Too often our emotions lead us to fight just for the sake of it. We may feel that an argument gives us a place to vent frustration about an issue we care deeply about but feel powerless to change, and we then falsely believe that "winning" an argument or shaming another for their views is somehow making the world a better place. If we find ourselves wanting a fight, pause and reset. If we realize that fighting is the goal, then it's best to step away.

Likewise, we are prone to enter conversations with the primary goal of impressing others. Here, our contributions to a discussion are less about enlightening others and more about shining a light on ourselves and promoting our own power, expertise, and authority. Whether we are actually experts on the matter or suffer from competency bias, others can usually sense when we are merely speaking for our own sake. "Mansplaining" falls into this category, where women experience the patronizing attitude of supposed male experts. Any kind of "splaining" is rarely helpful in any of the positive goals and objectives listed above.

Reflect

- How do you feel when someone tells you what you should think?
- Can you remember a time when you told someone what they should think? How did it impact your relationship?

Assess Potential Disagreement

Before or early in a discussion, assess the participants' agreement about the topics. This understanding helps us know what tools we need and what goals we can realistically achieve. Daniel Hallin, a professor of communications, developed a valuable rubric we can use to gauge potential disagreement.[7] He divides discussions into three concentric circles:

Sphere of Consensus

The inner circle contains discussions with either like-minded people or topics that have widespread agreement. Here, the conversation is typically more relaxed, but we shouldn't just assume that everyone thinks the same on every aspect of an issue. It's important to still carefully listen and consciously assess the level of agreement. There may be someone growing uncomfortable because they disagree with the group but don't know how to express it.

Even in the sphere of consensus, you should still use your best conversation skills and recognize that others have legitimate differences. Peacemaking involves refraining from using out-group labels or negative language toward people who believe differently, even if they aren't present in the discussion. Avoiding these two things makes everyone feel safer.

Sphere of Legitimate Controversy

The next outward circle contains topics spanning a wide range of belief, uncertainty, and disagreement. Some differences are mundane—for example, snowboarding versus skiing or a vacation at the beach versus in the mountains—but others have more practical importance. Hot-button issues may revolve around questions such as "What should public schools teach?" "What reproductive choices should a woman have?" and "How should we include LGBTQ people in society and the Church?" For con-

---

7. Daniel G. Hallin, *The Uncensored War, The Media and Vietnam*.

tentious issues like these, five people in a discussion may have five (or more) different and charged opinions.

Sphere of Deviance

Outside of the previous two circles is the sphere of deviance, where our shared reality is so minimal that we individually find it impossible to have a meaningful conversation. We may be polite, even curious, but these conversations rarely lead to someone changing their mind or learning something from the other. The lack of commonality defines whether the conversation is in the sphere of deviance. A topic that one person deems conspiratorial and extreme may be rational and believable to another. Individually we must decide whether a topic is in the sphere of deviance, regardless of how rational it is to the other person.

For example, I believe the earth is round, and if I were to talk with a flat-earther, that conversation would be in the sphere of deviance. But The Flat Earth Society,[8] which was founded in the early 1800s and is still alive today, has a robust membership, an active message board, and regular conventions. When flat-earthers talk among themselves, they are talking in the sphere of consensus.

Consider
• What topics do you place in the sphere of deviance?
• Remember some conspiracy theories are true. What conspiracy theories (in which powerful groups or people act in secret to harm others or enrich themselves) do you believe?

We don't need to engage in discussions in the sphere of deviance. But if we do, we still need to show dignity and respect. Labeling someone's beliefs as extremist or conspiratorial will alienate them. It's better to withdraw from the conversation than to discuss their beliefs with contempt.

These spheres change over time. Mónica Guzmán uses Hallin's spheres in her book *I Never Thought of it That Way*[9] and notes that when we are more politically divided, "the sphere of consensus shrinks . . . and the border between the sphere of legitimate discourse and the sphere of deviance

---

8. See The Flat Earth Society website.
9. Mónica Guzmán, *I Never Thought of It That Way: How to Have Fearlessly Curious Conversations in Dangerously Divided Times*, 52–53.

heaves, buckles, and breaks."[10] In today's polarized world, it's best to not assume consensus. We can only know if we ask.

Determine the Potential Cost

Before a difficult conversation, we need to be aware that we may pay a price for sharing our beliefs and making ourselves vulnerable to others' perceptions and actions. Expressing a different or opposing viewpoint may cause someone (even someone you consider to be part of your in-group) to think of you as an outsider, and it may even result in them subconsciously treating you with out-group bias. If so, they may become skeptical of you and your beliefs, even in areas where there had previously been agreement. This can happen in any group: in our quilting group, in our neighborhood, at work, at church, and within our own families.

Consider
• If others knew about some of your beliefs, would you have to pay a price? Is it a price you are unable or unwilling to pay?
• What beliefs do you have for which you are willing to pay a high price, including marginalization from your group?

Costs within Our Groups

At church we are not immune from bias and may subconsciously express it towards fellow members who think differently. Unknowingly, we sort and categorize people based on their beliefs. Some we think of as orthodox, true blue, nuanced, new convert, trustworthy, etc. Church leaders ask that we focus our ministerial efforts on helping people follow the covenant path and gain belief in core Church doctrine. We need a temple recommend to participate in temple ordinances, which requires approval by two priesthood leaders who ask questions about our beliefs and behaviors.[11] If we do not fully believe certain Church doctrine or live according to required behaviors, these leaders may refuse to authorize our temple recommend which prevents participation in temple worship.

With such strong forces toward common belief and behaviors within the Church and a natural tendency toward out-grouping, we may feel a strong bias against fellow Latter-day Saints who have or share different

---

10. Guzmán, 51.

11. See "Church Updates Temple Recommend Interview Questions," Newsroom.

religious or political beliefs. We expect strangers to think differently, but we may subconsciously suppose that all Latter-day Saints should have the exact same religious and political beliefs. It's usually not a big deal. But in some cases, people experience hurtful and traumatic marginalization.

Being ostracized at church unfortunately happens for both conservative and liberal beliefs. People have been released from callings and are no longer invited to speak in church simply because of their political opinions. Others have been called in to meet with their bishop to discuss concerns about the person's political positions and social media posts. This out-grouping sometimes extends to exclusion or marginalization of the person's children. It happens whenever there is difference in belief between someone and the group as a whole or its leaders. It is hurtful and it creates contention. However, just because it is natural does not mean we cannot overcome it.

Whatever group you may be in, whether it be at church, work, with friends, or with family, you must be aware of any potential price you might pay when expressing your views. At church, you may risk your reputation as a reliable follower of Jesus or your ability to serve in specific callings. You may suffer employment consequences. You may find yourself socially excluded in your neighborhood or with those who you thought were friends. In some sense you may be "cancelled."[12] None of these are reasons to remain silent if you feel you must speak up; however, it's important to choose carefully and be aware of possible fallout.[13]

Impact in Our Families

The most significant and impactful experiences we have occur in our families, and they are the most important groups to which we belong. Most families are filled with love and caring, but some are places of abuse and neglect. Even in families without dysfunction and direct harm, alienation can occur among family members who have different beliefs. My book *Bridges: Ministering to Those Who Question* describes what happens in a family when one of its members disaffiliates from the Church. Both believing and non-believing family members feel pain. The disaffiliating member often refuses to discuss their new beliefs with other family members because they don't think they will be accepted if the family really knew what they believed. Sadly, they are often right. Since religion and

---

12. Canceling is a phenomenon where someone is ostracized, loses privileges, or is boycotted because they say something that isn't acceptable to the group.

13. See chapter 8, where I illustrate different ways to minimize these costs.

politics are so connected in peoples' minds, this alienation occurs with political differences as well. I recently talked with a libertarian parent who wants to intervene because "her son is going down the rabbit hole into conservative politics." Another woman hasn't discussed politics with her father since 2010 and believes he would likely disown her if he knew her vote in the last presidential election.

If you are in this kind of family, my heart goes out to you. Practice self-care and protect your emotional health, and only disclose what is helpful to you. Even in these families, we have a responsibility to do what we can to create a family culture based on dignity.[14] Because our families are so much more important than other temporary and distant groups, our risk tolerance will be different. Some are willing to risk sharing their true thoughts, hoping their openness may be beneficial, while others are concerned about a potentially high price for their disclosure. There is no right answer, so consider your circumstances when wondering how much of your beliefs you should disclose to your family members.

Costs to Ourselves

Even when we are aware of our biases, we can't eliminate their effects in our own lives. At the same time, learning about others and their beliefs may change how we think about them. I talked with an immigration lawyer who works every day to help migrants who legally have the right to live in the United States. She believes that our immigration laws are intentionally designed to promote suffering and indignity, and she said that she doesn't want to know which of her ward members or neighbors supports child separation at the border or other *harsh* immigration policies. She said that she wants to love her ward members and would have a hard time feeling charitable about them if she knew they supported these things. Thus, to protect her relationships and feelings towards others, she has decided to avoid the topic in church and other related settings.

I also talked with a Church member who disagreed with the Church's position on vaccination and masking for COVID-19.[15] She felt negatively towards her ward members and leaders who she believed used public mask-

---

14. For specific skills that may be useful, see chapter 8, "Real life examples."

15. The Church issued a policy that, "To limit exposure to these viruses, we urge the use of face masks in public meetings whenever social distancing is not possible. To provide personal protection from such severe infections, we urge individuals to be vaccinated." See "The First Presidency Urges Latter-day Saints

ing and vaccination as a litmus test of their faithfulness to God. For her, masking and faithfulness are not equivalent. She lost trust in those who made this a condition of discipleship, and although she still participates in Church, she is hurt and skeptical of her ward leaders and members.

To Pay or Not to Pay

Each person should decide the price they want to pay in order to engage in certain conversations. In some settings, the price to participate in discussions about potentially contentious issues may be too high. It's okay to withdraw and be silent. But for some issues, we may be prepared to pay a high price, including marginalization from the groups we belong to, because the issue is so morally important to us. Change cannot occur when we are silent, nor if we are unprepared to pay.

Create the Right Setting

The success of our conversations also depends on their setting. Monica Guzmán identifies five critical elements for productive discussion: time, attention, parity, containment, and embodiment.[16] I add a sixth: consent.

- **Time**—Some topics take two minutes, but others take longer, hours even. We can connect and learn new information quickly, but we cannot have a thorough discussion to explore differences or to reach consensus without adequate time. Assess the time you have for the discussion prior to setting your goals to make sure you can have the discussion you want.

- **Attention**—Better conversations occur when all the parties are fully attentive in the discussion. When we are distracted, we tend to dismiss people and their opinions too quickly. If our discussions are on video call or phone, we may be prone to multitask, which prevents us from being fully present in the conversation. A Psychology Today article points out, "Research in neuroscience tells us that the brain doesn't really do tasks simultaneously, as we thought (hoped) it might. In fact, we just switch tasks quickly. Each time . . . a stop/start process goes on in the brain. That start/stop/start process is rough on us. Rather than saving time, it costs time (even very small microseconds). It's less effi-

to Wear Face Masks When Needed and Get Vaccinated Against COVID-19," First Presidency Message.

16. Guzmán, *I Never Thought of It That Way*, 84–86.

cient, we make more mistakes, and over time, it can sap our energy."[17] Even in person, it's disconnecting to see the other person checking their phone while half-listening to us. If a discussion is worth having, then it's worth paying attention. Put away the phones and turn off the TV; connecting is more important.

- **Parity**—If one person has power, or conversely, if one person has little power, that power imbalance means the person cannot be fully open, trusted, and engaged. In a presentation, the audience may ask questions, but the presenter has the power to decide what to talk about and how to interact with the audience. Full parity is required for controversial topics, including the power for participants to walk away from the discussion instead of feeling coerced into staying.

- **Containment**—Our conversations are more effective when we contain the discussion to those taking part—i.e., "what's said here stays here." We say things more openly and honestly when we are in a small and trusted setting. If the discussion is visible outside of those directly taking part, people will be (and should be) guarded in what they say. Social media is largely uncontained because, within the platform's privacy settings, others may be able to see and interact with our comments and discussion. Likewise, in large group settings, people may be uncomfortable sharing vulnerable experiences or beliefs that are unpopular with most of the group.

- **Embodiment**—Conversations online differ from those in person, where we can see people in real life—their gestures, facial expressions, and pauses—and can respond appropriately. Online is the least embodied, phone calls are good, video calls are better, and in person is best.

- **Consent**—Even if all the above characteristics are in place, it is inappropriate to discuss controversial issues when others do not want to. For example, Sunday school is a place where most participants want to study scripture and feel close to God. Someone who interrupts this expectation by wanting to discuss the politics of immigration may disrupt the meeting for others. Similarly, Thanksgiving dinner is a time to gather, share a meal, express gratitude, and build connections. Someone who insists on raising political issues, against the wishes of

---

17. Nancy K. Napier, "The Myth of Multitasking: Think you can multitask well? Think again."

others, disrupts and creates contention. Others may feel negatively towards the disruptor and their point of view. We need the consent of those participating to have productive discussions about potentially divisive issues. This can be achieved by simply asking something like, "Is it okay if we discuss. . ." and then fill in the topic.

Try

- Consider a future discussion you would like to have. What setting would you use?

Find and Use Reliable Information

Knowledge comes from accurate and reliable information. However, as President Dallin H. Oaks warns, that it isn't as easy as it sounds: "We live in a time of greatly expanded and disseminated information. We need to be cautious as we seek truth and choose sources for that search."[18] Although he was specifically talking about information surrounding our faith and religious matters, this same caution applies to information about any issues in our community.

We learn about issues through newspapers, television, radio, online publications, and social media. Decades ago, most news came through newspapers, which often had a partisan orientation. A large city usually had at least one liberal and one conservative newspaper. Newspapers published both news reports and editorials (when newspapers take a stand to advocate for positions on community issues and to endorse or oppose political candidates). Sometimes the boundaries blurred between the two. Newspapers were free to print what they wanted, within legal limits, but they were most often for-profit businesses that reported according to what best served their business and the interests of their owners—delivering what would net them the largest readership and the largest bottom line.

Due to the limited and finite radio and television frequencies available, in 1949 the Federal Communications Commission (FCC) established the Fairness Doctrine, which required radio or television broadcasters to "present fair and balanced coverage of controversial issues of interest to their communities, including by granting equal airtime to opposing candidates

---

18. Sydney Walker, "Watch: Be Cautious in Seeking Truth, President Oaks Says in New Video."

for public office."[19] This was to prevent one side from dominating available airwaves, and the FCC controlled broadcast access and made compliance a condition of receiving a television or radio license. Partly because of the rise of cable television, the government abolished the Fairness Doctrine in 1987, and broadcasters can now present any opinions or viewpoints, with no obligation to present both sides of contested issues.

Since 1987, news media has proliferated with cable, radio, and online reporting. This is unregulated, with each outlet choosing what fits their business model. They develop audience plans to attract viewers, listeners, and readers. Media sometimes reports opinion as though it is fact, making it hard to distinguish between fact and opinion. Some media have adopted the panel approach, with talking heads debating each other, resulting in what sometimes seems like a gladiator match. Other media outlets feature individual personalities on their own shows, presenting what they think will attract and build loyal viewers in order to sell advertising. Some shows build loyalty by discrediting other media as biased while hypocritically ignoring their own bias and inaccuracy in representing facts.

Some viewers become addicted to a particular channel, radio show, or website to get their news. Others get news from friends on social media as they post and discuss issues important to them. Still others turn it all off because it seems so angry, pointless, and impossible to sort through. They want to be good citizens and stay informed, but it seems impossible to find the truth.

If we want to understand today's issues and have meaningful discussions, we need a way to sift through media to find accurate and reliable information. Here are suggestions to sort through the noise:

- Evaluate the source with a level of skepticism related to how their messaging is geared to reach viewers, readers, or listeners in order to make money or increase power. Some media outlets make money based on outrage, vilification, or catastrophizing. Others make money based on attracting readers through in-depth and both-sides reporting. The best information is from media that doesn't activate our worst emotions.

  We must also come with a level of skepticism toward a source's bias and reliability. One helpful independent resource to evaluate media is Ad Fontes Media, which is a public benefit corporation funded through donations. You can search for "media bias and reliability" and view their assessment of a news source.

---

19. Matt Stefon, "Fairness Doctrine, United States Policy [1949–1987]."

- Read opposing information with an open mind. Opposing points of view are helpful if we are truly open to understanding why people may think differently. If we set aside our in-group and confirmation bias, we will see alternative ways of looking at an issue. We may even change our minds as we examine something from a new perspective, or we may better understand opposing positions and appreciate how someone may share them.

- Distinguish between fact and opinion. Although whether or not something is factual can be debated, facts are supposed to be proven by evidence, with the goal of objectivity. Opinions are interpretations and positions based on an individual's worldview and judgments. Some groups and individuals speak as though their opinions are fact. It may seem so to them, but since there are other ways to analyze and judge the same information, they are only expressing their opinions.

- Fact-check information. When we hear or read something that seems sensational, we can fact-check it to make sure it is being accurately reported. Certain websites track political claims and assess their accuracy. It's simple to fact-check: just type into your search engine the word "fact-check" and add in the issue. Explore the links to see what others say.

Try
• Evaluate the news media you use for reliability and bias by checking Ad Fontes Media or some other bias and reliability source. Did anything surprise you?
• Consider a claim that *your side* makes about a contemporary political issue that you aren't sure is right. Fact-check it. What did you find?

Prepare Emotionally

Some necessary conversations may be difficult because of strong and passionate disagreement. Use thoughtful planning to understand our objectives, assess the level of disagreement, and create the right setting. Consider our emotional state and the emotions the conversation may trigger in us. If we are angry or fearful, our judgment will not be clear, and we may need to defer the conversation.

When I wrote *Bridges: Ministering to Those Who Question*, I inter-
viewed mixed-faith couples and shared how one couple approaches difficult discussions:

> When a big issue comes up, Andrew gives Emily time to prepare before they
> discuss it. Emily said that when the Church's wealth drew a lot of public
> attention and news coverage, she knew Andrew would need to talk about
> it. They scheduled some time so Emily could emotionally prepare, and then
> Andrew and she were able to discuss it with mutual respect.[20]

If we jump into a hard conversation without preparation, we are less likely
to achieve our aim (even if we understand it in the first place).

Use the tools in this chapter to determine what you want out of the
conversation, the level of disagreement, and how to create the best setting
to achieve what you want. If we consciously try them several times (using
our rider), they will become natural and part of our subconscious models
(our elephant). Then we will use these tools frequently and effectively. Try
them. You will gain confidence in your ability to talk about difficult topics.

Book Group Questions

- Which tools are you looking forward to trying?
- Have you tried listening and being curious? What was the result?
- What challenges have you experienced when seeking reliable and accurate information?

---

20. David Ostler, *Bridges: Ministering to Those Who Question*, 169.

CHAPTER 7

Conversation Tools

The bridge between self and other is conversation: speaking and listening. When we speak, we tell others who and what we are. But when we listen, we allow others to tell us who they are. This is the supremely revelatory moment. And if we can't listen to other people, then we certainly can't listen to God.

—Rabbi Jonathan Sacks[1]

The previous chapter focused on first establishing a strong foundation on which to build a productive conversation. Now, just as various tools and materials are needed to build a house on a foundation, so too are the right tools needed to facilitate our discussions. This chapter focuses on what we can do during our conversations to make them effective and productive.

After a particularly challenging and difficult discussion, we may think to ourselves: *I shouldn't have said that; I should have said this.* In these conversations, our elephant and rider weren't in sync. Our subconscious elephant is instinctual, emotional, and reactive, responding at lightning speed. Our conscious rider is measured and thoughtful, but it needs time and energy to sort through the options. Our elephant was two steps ahead of us while our rider was looking back, wondering how we got to where we were.

By learning the tools in this chapter, we can be better equipped to step back from the brink and have more effective conversations when they become contentious. The tools are simple and memorable, and they will become natural with practice. They are summarized below, followed by detailed explanations of each.

- **Bring people into our group**—When we think about people being a part of our own group, we enhance conversational cohesion and reduce skepticism and negativity.

- **Dignify**—Using language and tone that dignify others both values them as people and shows respect.

- **Model good conversational techniques**—Through our words, body language, and attention we can show others we care about the conversation.

---

1. Jonathan Sacks, "Listen, Really Listen."

- **Obtain permission**—Determine whether our conversation partner is willing to hear what we want to say or answer our questions.

- **Ask curious questions**—If we want to really understand someone, we can ask them genuinely curious questions to learn about them and their perspectives.

- **Employ cognitive empathy**—When we use cognitive empathy to understand why someone believes as they do, we open avenues for discussion and learning.

- **Separate fact and opinion**—Agreeing on what are facts and what are opinions clarifies differences.

- **Use the Eavesdropper Test**—Consider how someone secretly listening to our conversation would feel.

- **Try the Ideological Turing Test**—How well do we understand another's views? This tool tests whether we can describe someone else's ideology and belief in a way that the other person would agree is accurate.

- **Find agreement and common ground**—Our conversations can be more meaningful when we understand where we have agreement.

- **Pause**—Sometimes it is helpful to stop a conversation and reframe it or take a moment catch our breath.

- **Discussing conspiracy theories**—There are ways to discuss conspiracy theories that are helpful and productive.

- **End or withdraw**—Choose when to end a conversation, either because it has reached a healthy point, or because it is headed for contention.

Let's look at each of these tools in detail.

Bring People into Our Group

In-group and out-group biases have been mentioned throughout this book because they are a big reason for contention. They are also relatively easy to address, at least in principle; after all, a key solution to these—*in-grouping*—is part of our theology. As Latter-day Saints, we believe we are all part of one great eternal human family. We know our heavenly parents love us and have a plan for us to return to them. God commands us, "Ye shall not esteem one flesh above another, or one man shall not think himself above another" (Mosiah 23:7).[2] Implicit in our covenants is our promise to help everyone feel love, including those who believe things differently than us, and so in-grouping is a way to extend that love by consciously pulling others into our circle. While the concept is simple, it is hard in practice. Some groups of people are so different that it may be difficult to see or feel commonality, and some groups we may really not like. Our natural tendency for out-group bias fosters negativity against those we may view as other.

We don't need to be slaves to this natural bias. With conscious effort we can find ways to in-group. In particular, we can use language that helps bring others into our group. For example, use *we* and *us*, instead of *they* and *them*. Highlight agreement when you find it, and use positive labels instead of negative ones. Whenever and wherever we encounter people who think or act differently, we must extend love and respect. Every perceived political or religious enemy is fully human and should be treated with dignity and love. If we can do this, our perspective changes. We find ourselves more open to understanding where they are coming from and why they believe what they do.

Ponder
• What out-groups are hardest for you to respect?
• How would you *in-group* them? Do you want to?
• How can you help others *in-group* you?

Dignify

In a 2017 Newsroom commentary, the Church stated, "From its beginning in the womb to its final breath, and at each stage in between, every human life is endowed with dignity. . . . As Rabbi Sacks said, 'We cannot love God without first honoring the universal dignity of humanity as the image and likeness of the universal God.'"[3] Donna Hicks, an expert in international conflict management, calls dignity "an internal state of peace that comes with the recognition and acceptance of the value and

---

2. President Gordon B. Hinckley teaches, "We have an obligation to reach out beyond ourselves to help those in distress and trouble and difficulty where they may be." Gordon B. Hinkley, *Stand a Little Taller*, 329. See also Lloyd D. Newell, "'All Are Alike unto God': Equality and Charity in the Book of Mormon," 196–210.

3. "The Dignity of Human Life," Newsroom.

vulnerability of all living things."[4] To dignify is to think of others' value during our conversations. It does not require shared views; instead, it recognizes when others come to the conversation legitimately and with good faith. It is to acknowledge that they are divine with an eternal personality, unique genetics, and life experiences that lead them to different opinions. By valuing this uniqueness, we open ourselves to learning from their perspectives and experiences as we exchange ideas with them.

While we cannot measure our feelings of dignity toward others, we can evaluate the dignity (or lack of it) in our language. Unite, a non-profit that helps reduce division and solve community problems, developed The Dignity Index to rate how specific communications dignify others on an eight-point scale:[5]

1. Feels the other side is less than human and calls for or approves violence.

2. Accuses the other side not just of doing bad or being bad but of promoting evil.

3. Attacks the other side's moral character, not just their capabilities or competence.

4. Mocks and attacks the other side's background, beliefs, commitment, competence, or performance.

5. Listens to the other side's point of view and respectfully explains their own goals, views, and plans.

6. Sees it as a welcome duty to work with the other side to find common ground and act on it.

7. Wants to fully engage the other side—discussing the deepest disagreements to see what breakthroughs they can find.

8. Sees self as part of every group, and by refusing to hate anyone, offers dignity to everyone.

Using language that shows dignity may initially seem perfunctory, but the more we use it, the more we will feel connected to the other person. We become curious and respect that others may think and believe differently than us. We see others not as enemies, but as people who have value.

---

4. Donna Hicks, *Dignity: Its Essential Role in Resolving Conflict*, 20.
5. See The Dignity Index website.

Evaluate
• If researchers evaluated your conversations, what level on The Dignity Index would they find most often? • What one small change could you make to try to level up?

Model Good Conversational Techniques

A conversation is like a dance. It has a tempo and rhythm, moving back and forth. When we start, we don't know exactly how it will progress, what the pace will be, or where it will end. The first person sends the conversation in a particular direction, then others redirect it as they respond. Each person feeds off the other as they talk, listen, ask questions, and plan their next steps. The movement of the conversation is dynamic with a life of its own, carrying all participants together. If one person tenderly expresses something accompanied by tears, others' hearts might open, and they may express themselves with sympathetic tears. Likewise, if one's conversation is contentious, negative and judgmental, others may respond in kind.

Subconsciously, we mirror the emotions and actions of others. After all, elephants are herd animals, and we humans travel together in groups. Here are a few tips for good conversations. By using them, other conversationalists will be more likely to follow our lead:

- **Always be present.** This means being fully engaged in the conversation. It shows in our eyes and body language. Avoid looking away, using a phone, multitasking, or giving into other distractions that take us away from what the other person is saying.

- **Use affirming body language.** A large part of communication is nonverbal. We can use our body to show our interest. We can lean slightly forward, nod in affirmation, have a relaxed posture, and keep our eyes on the other person. When this is hard for us, we can practice until it becomes natural and infectious.

- **Repeat back what is heard.** One way to listen well is to summarize what we hear. This makes sure we understand what is said. It also helps others know that we are genuinely trying to understand their point of view.

- **Pull people into our circle.** We are social creatures and treat those in our group more charitably. By using "we" and "us" in our conversations, we pull people into our group and create more openness and kindness. When necessary, we can use neutral terms, such as "that belief" or "one's belief" instead of "your belief."

- **Admit the faults of our own group.** As stated earlier, every group has faults—whether they be churches, political parties, or groups of like-minded friends. We are more honest when we admit our side has its own extremists, has made mistakes, and has some positions without complete agreement throughout the group. Acknowledging this sets a pattern to help others be open to their own humanness and mistakes; everyone then becomes more open to learning.

- **Extend charity.** Even when we believe our discussion partner's opinion is wrong and harmful, we need not let that define how we see them. None of us wants to be wholly judged by our worst opinions, beliefs, or actions. Recognize this for others and know that they also have many well-formed opinions and many aspects of goodness within them.

Reflect

- Which of these six positive conversation practices are natural for you?
- What changes do you want to make?

For all of these, sincerity is absolutely crucial. When we are sincere, these behaviors show our openness, interest, and concern for others. These behaviors create trust—not some artificial, manufactured trust, but genuine trust and partnership. In good dancing, partners trust each other and are unified as they create a beautiful spectacle. It's the same in conversations.

Likewise, negative behaviors adversely affect our discussions, rippling through and changing the interaction. Some negative behaviors that weaken our relationships with others include:

- **Name-calling, vilifying, or "other-izing."** Be thoughtful when referring to people who think differently. This applies even when they are not present. Use terms that extend grace and charity. Don't call people apostates, wayward, enemies, brainwashed, ignorant, blind followers, or any term that characterizes them in a derogatory way. Avoid today's polarizing political terms including fascist, Marxist, right-wing nutjob, left-wing nutjob, radical, crazy, and so forth. This puts others in an out-group and makes it harder to understand them.

- **Disparaging opposing views as stupid or ignorant.** Others' points of view may be incorrect or incomplete, but they likely sincerely come from their own personal worldview and experience. Instead, try to understand the path that took them to their opinion. Regardless of whether we agree with the destination, we can try to understand and respect their thinking.

- **Raising your voice.** Yelling, screaming, or typing in ALL CAPS will probably invite a similar response. If others do that with us, respond by turning the other cheek and moving the conversation to higher ground.

- **Dominating, manipulating, or coercing.** Nothing destroys trust like using tricks or power to get our way, even in conversations. Some try to get their way by asking leading questions or using family, church, or community authority, and it is almost always unrighteous. In the scriptures God warns us that "when we . . . exercise control or dominion or compulsion . . . the heavens withdraw themselves; the Spirit of the Lord is grieved" (D&C 121:37).

Consider
• Which of these four negative conversation practices are easy for you to avoid?
• If you want to be a better listener, which areas would you want to improve?

Can you imagine a dance in which one dancer tries to trick the other into doing all the right moves, dominating the flow, tempo, and dance moves on the floor? One dancer may lead, but they do not dominate. Good dancers dance together and trust each other. When we master productive conversation tactics and avoid destructive ones, the conversation moves with thoughtful consideration and respect for the other. Our partners are then more likely to trust us, mirror our moves, and remain open to meaningful discussion.

Obtain Permission

This is a simple but powerful technique. By asking for permission before presenting a question or offering our opinion, we demonstrate respect and avoid imposing our views on others. This helps slow down the pace of the conversation and allows everyone involved to consider the tone and nature of the discussion more carefully. When others give their consent, they become more receptive to considering our questions and opinions. It is easy to implement this technique; simply ask, "Would it be okay if I offered my thoughts?" or "Do you mind if I ask a question?"

Ask Curious Questions

When in doubt, ask a question. Questions themselves are one of the best ways to accomplish our discussion goals. Whether building relationships, trying to understand an issue, coming to a common agreement, or trying to change someone's mind, effective questions can help us achieve our objectives. As *Preach My Gospel*—the guide for LDS missionaries—notes, questions were a key way in which the Savior engaged others: "Jesus Christ often asked questions to help people ponder and apply principles. His questions prompted thought, soul searching, and commitment. Good questions will help you understand interests, concerns, or questions that others have."[6]

Jim Henderson and Jim Hancock are Christian ministers who developed a structured way to hold meaningful conversations about divisive topics. One of their principles is: "I'll have unusual interest in others." Their method is called 3Practices, which involves convening groups of people (such as associates at work, church, or school, or sometimes even complete strangers) who get together in person or by video to talk about a difficult topic. They call the group a 3Practice Circle, which focuses on a single topic. An individual takes about two minutes to express their opinion, and then anyone can ask a question—but (here is the catch) it must begin with the phrase "I'd be curious to know . . ."[7]

This approach activates one's interest and inquisitiveness. It helps people focus on understanding one another and identifying questions to help them understand even more. Curiosity pulls others into our group because they know we are interested. Being curious eliminates the tendency to listen with skeptical thinking and opens our minds and hearts to what others are saying. Our conscious cognition becomes active while calming our subconscious elephant, and we create a more open and reasoned conversation.

The best questions help participants understand another's opinion and life experience, why they think the way they do, and sometimes critically examine their own position. Asking "I'd be curious to know . . ." opens both parties to greater engagement and sincerity. Every participant

---

6. *Preach My Gospel*, 185.

7. See the 3Practices website.

can learn this simple skill, and it can quickly become part of their subconscious cognition.

Examples of "I'd Be Curious to Know" Questions

- I'd be curious to know how you would secure our borders.
- I'd be curious to know how you think your life would be different if you were born a different race.
- I'd be curious to know what you are afraid will happen to your family now that your daughter has stopped attending church.
- I'd be curious to know whether you think political correctness has gone too far.

Again, sincerity is crucial. To be effective, these questions need to be genuinely curious toward understanding their minds and their worldviews. We must want to learn and help others fully reflect on their positions. It's a beautiful dance: everyone feels closer and is elevated. The novelist Thea Astley says it well: "The more you try to be interested in other people, the more you find out about yourself."[8]

It's also crucial to be conscious of our intent and to not manipulate someone with our questions. A manipulative question uses force or trickery to corner another into answering in a particular way. It's a "gotcha" question that makes the other person feel trapped into agreement; it creates out-grouping instead of openness and honesty. While such questions may give us the answers we want to hear, they ultimately result in feigned responses and feelings of distrust that push others further away. The best questions help you understand others or cause reflection and openness. Manipulative questions seldom do so.

Examples of Manipulative Questions

- I'm sure you agree that . . . right?
- Every good person knows . . . Why do you believe . . . ?
- It's obvious that . . . How can you not see that?

---

8. Thea Astley was an Australian author who published dozens of books between 1960 and her death in 2004. This quote is frequently used as an inspirational saying but is unsourced. I chose to include it without a full source because it makes the point so clearly that curiosity about others enriches us.

Use Cognitive Empathy

Empathy means to understand the *feelings* of others. Cognitive empathy is to understand *what other people believe* and *why they believe it*. In some ways, it's similar to dancers who know their partners so well they know their every signal, skill, and move.

We should aspire to understand others so we know where they are coming from. Chapter 2 discussed an experiment involving a researcher dipping a sterilized cockroach into apple juice and then offering the juice to participants to drink. Those who wouldn't drink the juice first subconsciously felt disgust, and then used their conscious thinking to explain what their subconscious cognition had already decided. The conscious cognition comes *after* the subconscious. So it is with many, if not most, of our beliefs. We subconsciously believe something, then create reasoned arguments to support that belief. The elephant goes where it wants, and then the rider explains later why they wanted to go exactly where the elephant did.

According to Jonathan Haidt, our subconscious cognition arrives at its decision based on the relative importance of the values we hold.[9] In the cockroach and apple juice case, our deeply embedded desire for purity and cleanliness is almost hard-wired in our bodies to keep us safe from disease and parasites. Our subconscious thinking thus helps us quickly come to a belief based on our underlying values, without needing to evaluate each occurrence on their own. Our rational minds can overcome it sometimes, but as the experiment showed, participants still wouldn't drink the apple juice after rationally being shown it was safe.

To understand why someone believes what they do, we must first understand how they arrived at their belief. This process comes from one's epistemology—the "framework for sorting out what is true"[10]— i.e., how we come to know what we know. Here are some possible epistemological categories:[11]

---

9. Jonathan Haidt, *The Righteous Mind: Why Good People Are Divided by Politics and Religion*, 3–31.

10. David McRaney, *How Minds Change: The Surprising Science of Belief, Opinion, and Persuasion*, 96. He further elaborates, "Epistemology is about translating evidence into confidence. By taking what we believe then sorting through some kind of system for arranging, organizing, and classifying it against the available evidence, our certainty in truth should go up or down." McRaney, 97. Understanding what system someone used to sort through their information is critical to understanding the other person.

11. Peter Boghossian and James Lindsay, *How to Have Impossible Conversations, A Very Practical Guide*, 60. There are likely other epistemologies, but this

- **Feelings**—I know it is true in my heart.
- **Culture**—It's what everyone knows is true.
- **Religion**—It's taught that way in scripture or church.
- **Reason**—Logical, conscious thinking shows it to be.
- **Evidence**—There are sufficient facts to prove it.

Since our worldviews are unique, so too are our epistemologies. If we learn that someone who believes that abortion is murder was nearly aborted themselves by their mother, we may see a completely different epistemology than someone who believes abortion should be illegal because of their religious beliefs about conception and the human soul. They arrived at the same conclusion—anti-abortion—but through different epistemologies.

Likewise, a Reform Jew may be pro-choice because of her religious beliefs, and an emergency room nurse may treat a child raped by her father and believe that the victim should be able to end a pregnancy. Both the Reform Jew and the nurse arrived at the same conclusion—pro-choice—but, again, through different epistemologies.

David McRaney highlights the importance of exploring epistemology so that we may be more conscious of how we and others know what we know. If we approach a potentially difficult discussion with cognitive empathy, we can gain "an understanding that what others experience as the truth arrives in their minds unconsciously" and recognize that "arguments over conclusions are often a waste of time. The better path . . . would be for both parties to focus on their processing, on *how* and *why* they see what they see, not what."[12]

Cognitive empathy takes effort. Hugo Mercier, a cognitive scientist, writes, "For me to be able to anticipate why you might disagree with me, I would have to do a lot of cognitive work. Because you've got a lot of beliefs I don't have, and it would be very hard for me to anticipate why you might think as you do."[13] Some simple tools to increase cognitive empathy to better understand someone's thought process are:

- **Ask whether they have always thought so.** You could ask, "Did you always think that COVID-19 vaccination is safe and effective?" or "Has your belief changed about the fairness of the election?" If the person expresses their beliefs have changed, you can follow up with "What has

framework is illustrative of the many ways someone can come to a belief.

12. McRaney, *How Minds Change*, 86.
13. McRaney, 190.

changed?" This can both give you a good clue into their epistemology and provide you a chance to reflect on your own.

- **Assess someone's certainty.** Ask a question like, "On a scale of 1 to 10, how likely are you to get vaccinated for COVID-19?" or "How certain are you that the election was fair?" These questions open the answers to a range of possibilities, instead of just a yes or a no.

- **Ask if anything could change their certainty.** If they express that they are hesitant about vaccines, you could ask, "Can you think of anything that would change your feelings about getting vaccinated?" Or you could offer specific information that, if true, would change their minds, such as, "If you knew that Donald Trump believed he lost the election but refused to admit it publicly, would that change your certainty about the fairness of the election?" This gives you additional information to understand how they interpret information.

- **Reevaluate your conversation goals.** If your conversational goal is to change someone's mind, and they express with 100% certainty that a secret group of high-level US governmental officials planned and carried out the 9/11 attacks, not al-Qaeda (for me this a long since debunked belief), then you should change your goal. You aren't likely to persuade them. Instead you can focus your discussion on something productive, or you can just walk away.

When we exercise cognitive empathy, we find that two things happen. First, our conversations have better content and tone. Our discussion partner doesn't feel they have to *defend* their belief; they simply need to *describe* it. They can also be more vulnerable in the certainty of their beliefs. Second, we better understand our own certainty, which makes us open to understanding where our beliefs come from and the ways they might be incomplete.

Practice

- Pick a societal or political belief. Can you identify the epistemology that led you to that belief? That is, how did you come to believe what you believe?
- Have you always thought that? What has changed?
- How certain are you of that belief?
- Is there anything that would cause you to reevaluate your certainty?

Separate Fact and Opinion

As discussed in the previous chapter, relying on good information is crucial to having a productive conversation. However, the blurring of facts, opinions, and falsehoods in our media, and the battle over what constitutes each, can make discussions relying on facts difficult. With this in mind, it can be helpful to step back and distinguish between what is agreed on (facts) and what is disagreed on (opinions). This eliminates confusion and highlights the basis for disagreement. Then we can work together to address it.

This can be done by asking, "On a scale of 1 to 10, how certain are you that . . . ?" and following up with, "Is there any information that would change your level of certainty?" If the other person is open, a follow-up question might be, "Should we try to find that information?" or "I've heard . . . I'd be curious to know whether this is information you are interested in." These questions show whether their certainty is so strong that more information isn't helpful or help us learn the right kind of new information that would be helpful to them.

These tools require sensitivity. People are receptive to new information when they decide they want new information—not when they are told their beliefs are wrong. When we fact-check people, we put them on the defensive. Telling others what we think are the *facts,* when they aren't open to considering them, rarely changes minds and often creates interpersonal alienation. The context and setting matters. The power of group identity and bias contributes to our skepticism when we hear and consider new information. Thus, some are less open when the source of the new information is someone they don't trust.

Constant fact-checking is especially counterproductive. It's irritating to be told we are wrong, which can make us feel cornered and defensive. Then it is harder to change beliefs. If we are the person who knows everything and always points out mistaken ideas, we become the enemy and a part of the out-group. We become the belief police, and everyone runs for cover whenever we are around. If we want to be the belief police, it's best to do it within our *own side* where others will be more open to considering our point of view.

Most of us seek truth, and growth only occurs when we are open and willing to consider alternatives. Thus, in the right setting and with the right emotional willingness to learn, we revise our beliefs when presented with opposing information.

Consider

- Do you have any political beliefs of which you aren't completely certain?
- What information would increase or decrease your certainty?
- What sources do you trust to give you reliable information that could change your certainty?
- What sources don't you trust?

Use the Eavesdropper Test

This test exposes the conversational equivalent of gossip, when we say unkind things behind someone's back but kinder things to their face. The same thing often happens between groups. When speaking with individuals who share our beliefs, we are more likely to resort to name-calling, stereotyping, and making assumptions about the intentions and knowledge of those who hold opposing views. This reinforces a false and negative image of those who think differently that can unintentionally leak out in conversation as contempt.

To address this problem, the Eavesdropper Test asks us to imagine that individuals who hold different views are listening in on our conversations. This can help us evaluate whether we are fairly representing them and their positions, as well as whether we are using language that is dignifying and respectful. If we find that we are not, we know that we need to make changes. We cannot be peacemakers by saying unkind things about other groups to like-minded friends, or even under our breath to ourselves. Healing our divides means changing the way we see others and making that change heart-deep. This exercise teaches us not only how to have more respectful discussions but also how to respect others when they are not around.

Articulate Others' Beliefs

The Turing Test was proposed by Alan Turing, a mathematician and computer scientist, as a means to test a computer's ability to exhibit intelligent behavior indistinguishable from a human's. The test involves individuals engaging in a blind conversation with both another person and a computer. If they are unable to tell which responses came from the person and which came from the computer, then the computer has passed the test.

The Ideological Turing Test has been adapted from the original to measure how well people can describe another's ideology.[14] It is done by attempting to articulate the other person's arguments in a way that someone wouldn't know that you didn't believe in that ideology. To succeed, you need to understand the position *as they understand it*—including the underlying facts they are assuming and the rationale they are applying. That understanding only comes by asking sincere and curious questions. Debaters often use this tool, because in some debate competitions, they are assigned to advocate for a certain side. That means they must arrive at the competition having prepared persuasive arguments for both sides, regardless of their personal stance on the issue. Try this tool in your next conversation with someone who believes differently.

Find Agreement and Common Ground

We have a great deal in common with everyone around us. Even when we have significant political or religious disagreements, our common ground likely outweighs our areas of difference. This is an important truth that can help us avoid contention. At church, I have served and worshipped with others who have a desire to serve God, build a happy family life, and love their neighbors. Their political views have only become apparent when I see bumper stickers or yard signs telling me that they either differ from or share my political ideology. I've seen it as I have lived, worked, and served out of the United States in the United Kingdom, Sierra Leone, Japan, and India. In all these settings, I've seen that most people love their families, try to live a moral life, and hope for a fair and just world. With all we have in common, it's hard to imagine that we can't find a way to be friends with those who support a different political candidate.

Even when we disagree on an important topic, there is usually at least some aspect of the topic where we can find agreement. There is always common ground, and the act of finding it reduces contention. Finding common ground helps us see others as our in-group and helps remove out-group bias. When we think about our commonalities, we are more open to considering others' issues and concerns. It's easy to do this; just ask, "What do you think we agree on about this issue?"

Finding shared ground brings us together. The social scientist Arthur C. Brooks says, "Focus on what unites us—our shared values—rather

---

14. Bryan Caplan, "The Ideological Turing Test."

than just our own side's *expression* of shared values. When we start with the shared values themselves, we establish common moral ground, which then allows us to talk in a spirit of respect about our disagreement in the most effective way to express these values. Even without agreement, it strikes a blow against contempt."[15]

Try This

- Sit down with a friend with whom you disagree with on a topic.
- Say, "I know we disagree about (fill in the blank) but probably not everything about it. I'd like to see if there are areas where we agree."

Pause

Since conversations are dynamic, pauses are helpful to assess where we are. It gives us a chance to reset. We can pause by simply saying something like, "Okay if I pause for a moment? I want to respond thoughtfully, and pausing helps me clarify my thinking." This can do a few things: it breaks the flow and activates conscious cognition; it signals respect and tells others that we want to be thoughtful, letting them do the same; and it slows down the pace of the conversation so that it is less likely to veer off into contention. These pauses also provide time to use our conscious reasoning, and to go back to our blueprints and design tools and make sure we are clear on our objectives and our alignment with others. After pausing, if we still sense a mismatch between the aim and the actual conversation, we can say, "Just thinking about our conversation, this is what I would like to get out of our discussion. What about you?"

If we feel anger, fear, or other intense emotions, it is time to step away. While these are legitimate feelings, such powerful emotions do not usually serve us well when we want to have meaningful discourse. As authors Peter Boghossian and James Lindsay point out, "Anger blinds you and derails conversations . . . Anger [is] a strong cognitive bias that pushes you to confirm your anger is justified. Anger leads you to misinterpret information that might cause you to feel anything other than angry."[16] Jesus also condemned anger, proclaiming that "whosoever is angry with his brother shall be in danger of the judgment" (Matt. 5:22, Joseph Smith Translation).

---

15. Arthur C. Brooks, *Love Your Enemies: How Decent People Can Save America from the Culture of Contempt*, 100.

16. Boghossian and Lindsay, *How to Have Impossible Conversations*, 124.

When we feel anger or some other strong emotion that clouds our judgment, we can say, "I feel this is getting a little heated. Is it okay if we take a five-minute break and come back after it dissipates?" or "I'm feeling angry; let's pick this up tomorrow after my anger passes." Remember that intense emotions like anger affect us physically as our bodies release hormones that increase our blood pressure and heart rate, impacting our subconscious cognition.[17] We can't mentally stop its effects and may need time for the adrenaline to dissipate and our heart rate to return to normal. It is okay to give ourselves permission to feel our feelings—including anger—and take time to process them personally to avoid derailing our discussion. Such a pause may be just for a moment, several minutes, or even days. Communicating the need for a pause is key so that we are not leaving our conversation partners hanging unnecessarily.

When anger drives our subconscious cognition, it is most often destructive, especially when we react in our passion. People who are blinded by anger can strike out in verbal or physical violence, destroying lives and relationships. In some circumstances, however, after our conscious mind is in control, anger can motivate us to seek change in ourselves or fix injustice and unfairness. This anger isn't reactive and in the moment; instead, it is used as a part of conscious thought to productively channel these emotions.

Ways to Pause a Conversation

- "Can we pause and reflect for a moment so I can respond thoughtfully?"
- "I want to talk about this. Can we find a better time to discuss it?"
- "I know little about that. Can you give me a few days so I can have a meaningful discussion with you?"

Discussing Conspiracy Theories

As discussed in the previous chapter, conspiracy theory is a belief that a powerful group is secretly working together to harm society, gain power, or enrich themselves.[18] Some conspiracy theories are true, but most are not. Some are provable, but many are inherently disprovable when the conspiracy itself involves the powerful group manipulating and obscuring the *real* information. Thus, the lack of evidence can be viewed as proof of the conspiracy.

---

17. See "Emotional bias" in Chapter 3.
18. See "Conspiratorial thinking" in chapter 3.

These theories can be dangerous and can undermine trust in our important institutions, and it's important to see through them and discuss them with others. Here are five simple steps for discussing conspiracy theories:

- **Be careful about terminology.** While the actual definition of a conspiracy theory is neutral, the words "conspiracy" and "conspiracy theory" often have negative connotations and may evoke a defensive reaction. Applying the label in our mind without verbalizing it also affects our subconscious approach to the issue. Instead, treat it simply as a belief, asking and discussing it in the same way you would any other belief. Believing conspiracy theories isn't a sign of being stupid. In the past we know that government leaders have intentionally conspired and lied to the public to keep the country in war, and all too often we learn of business leaders conspiring to avoid or lie about safety regulations in order to increase profits. Because of this reality, all of us likely believe at least one conspiracy theory. There are social and cognitive reasons that lead us to be attracted to them. If we show contempt, we alienate the other and likely entrench their beliefs.

- **Use cognitive empathy.** Ask questions about how others came to their belief, including their epistemology.[19] Remember that when people explain their belief, they often become more certain in it. It's better to ask *how* they came to the belief rather than *what* they believe. Since conspiracy theories are often attractive to people who are alienated from society or have low trust in specific institutions such as science, religion, or government, pay attention to epistemologies and experiences pointing to that lack of trust.

- **Assess their certainty.** Asking how certain they are about their belief using a 1 to 10 scale is helpful. Our subsequent discussion will be different if they have a 10 in certainty than if they say 5. Follow up by asking whether anything could make them more or less certain. If yes, explore it and ask how they could find that information.

- **Ask questions to assess the breadth of conspiracy.** Many conspiracy theories require hundreds or thousands of people to be involved in the conspiracy. The more people who must keep the conspiracy secret, the more likely it is to be exposed. You can ask, "How many insiders are involved? How do they keep it secret?" These questions won't disprove the theory, but they may give pause and cause reconsideration over time.

---

19. See "Use cognitive empathy" in chapter 6.

- **Don't expect to change their belief.** You probably won't change their mind. But sometimes their subconscious will feel uncertain because of your conversation, and it may lead to their reconsideration later.

It is essential to learn how to productively take on these tough conversations because the widespread adoption of conspiracy theories can be corrosive and can undermine our trust in each other and in important societal institutions. Such theories are growing in number and are increasingly impacting us negatively. With the right tools, we can engage productively in difficult conversations about conspiracy theories.

End or Withdraw

Healing our divides does not mean that we must engage in every discussion. There are times when it may be best to be silent or to withdraw from a conversation. When your find yourself in a potentially contentious discussion, you don't have to participate. Use these considerations to decide whether to continue with the conversation or to withdraw:

- **Time**—Make sure that you have adequate time. Make sure that you don't take time away from higher priorities such as work, family, and other personal priorities.

- **Energy**—If you don't have enough emotional and mental energy, you won't be able to check your bias or use your best skills. If you are tired and want to have an important but potentially contentious discussion, reschedule. Wait to engage until you are at your physical and mental best.

- **Cost**—Disclosing your beliefs may carry a cost, including marginalization and loss of status or respect. You should consider whether you want to or are able to pay that cost before entering into a conversation where you might choose to share your belief in something unpopular.

- **Good discussion environment**—In some circumstances, it's not possible to have productive discussions. Assess the environment to make sure you can positively participate, or that you can shape the environment to make it positive.

If you decide you can't or don't want to participate, you can withdraw from the conversation, or reschedule it to when you have the time and energy to engage. If you can't leave the conversation, you can just remain silent. You can set boundaries and only participate in a way that is helpful to you.

There are other tools; if you find one, use it. I've only included these basic ones, which all of us can use without advanced degrees or extensive training. As we master these simple tools, very few conversations become contentious. Use the skills from this chapter, find out which ones work for you, and practice them so they are in your subconscious mental drawer of tools. When you need them, your subconscious elephant will automatically use them. You'll be surprised at how well they work.

Book Group Questions

- Which tools are you looking forward to trying?

- Have you tried to understand someone else's epistemology for something on which you disagree? Could you pass the Ideological Turing Test?

- Pick an area of disagreement among members of the book group. Can you find common ground about that issue?

CHAPTER 8

Real Life Examples

Thing is, we have to really be careful about who we hate. Because 10 times out of 10, it's going to be somebody Jesus loves.

—Beth Moore[1]

To bridge divides . . . we need to put our curiosity to work—minding the gaps between what we know and what we don't, collecting knowledge that inspires different questions, charging ahead on the most complicated issues, and not letting lazy, easy answers suffice.

—Mónica Guzmán[2]

Let's now put these tools into practice. In this chapter there are examples of potentially contentious situations to explore how the principles and tools from the two previous chapters can be best utilized.

Discussing Religious Beliefs in a Family

It's Sunday family dinner with parents and their three adult children. Their twenty-five-year-old daughter Lindsay lives in Denver and is in town on business for the week. Everyone is excited to see her since she only comes to town a few times a year. Dad knows Lindsay has been distant from the Church, but for the first time, he notices she isn't wearing temple garments.[3] He feels responsible for the spirituality of his family and wants to help Lindsay through whatever faith challenges she is having. Dad feels almost compelled to bring it up. As the food is being passed, he says, "Lindsay, why are you no longer wearing garments?"

Let's step back and evaluate Dad's approach.

- **Setting**—How would we rate the setting for this conversation using the six elements discussed in chapter 6?

  o *Time:* High. They have all evening to talk.

---

1. Beth Moore (@BethMoreLPM), "Thing is, we have to really be careful about who we hate."

2. Monica Guzmán, *I Never Thought of It That Way: How to Have Fearlessly Curious Conversations in Dangerously Divided Times*, 71.

3. Garments are specific underwear worn by adult adherents of The Church of Jesus Christ of Latter-day Saints who have participated in the endowment ordinance in one of its temples. See "Garments," Gospel Topics.

o *Attention:* High. Dinner with family is typically a social setting where everyone is facing each other and expected to converse.

o *Parity:* Low. A parent always has a degree of parental authority, even with adult children.

o *Containment:* Low. While dinner usually involves an expectation for conversation, it is also a very difficult setting to leave. With the whole family looking on, Lindsay may be uncomfortable discussing her religious beliefs, particularly if she knows that they will disappoint the parents. Because Lindsay is staying at her parents' house, pressing this issue may cause her to feel trapped.

o *Embodiment:* High. Everyone participates in person.

o *Consent:* Lindsay hasn't agreed to discuss her personal religious beliefs, let alone her underwear. She may be concerned that if she was honest, it could negatively affect her relationships or her status in her family.

- **Objective**—Dad wants his family to remain close and share common religious beliefs, and he worries for Lindsay's own spirituality. He is fearful that if Lindsay doesn't believe in the Church, they may not be together eternally.[4] Dad wants to listen and understand what Lindsay believes so he can help her change. He feels strongly that he must get this issue out in the open, not knowing exactly where it will go.

Dad's elephant (subconscious cognition), perhaps motivated by fear and other strong emotions, has him charging forward without thinking about whether this is the right setting for this discussion. Not only could it easily end in tears and contention, but it may also alienate his relationship with Lindsay and even other family members. She might take offense that he wants to talk about her religious beliefs—and her underwear!—especially in front of the family. She may feel that her parents are treating her like a child and that they don't trust or honor her ability to make her own decisions.

In *Bridges: Ministering to Those Who Question*, I write how uncommon it is for people who are experiencing a faith crisis to confide in family members and friends about their concerns and doubts. They worry about being misunderstood, misjudged, or losing relationships that are important to them. Instead, they tend to only express their concerns to those

---

4. Latter-day Saints believe that families live together after this life if they are faithful to Church teachings and practices.

who will listen without judgment and where there is little risk to important relationships such as family. Even when they disclose their concerns or own beliefs, they may be wary and only share a small part at first while evaluating whether it is safe to express more. They understand that they may have to pay some cost by being honest, including enduring judgment, losing trust and status, or even damaging family relationships.[5]

What are other ways Dad might have used to approach this situation?

- **Build the relationship; learn and listen.** If Dad's goal is to strengthen his relationship, he could start this conversation before dinner by privately saying something like, "Lindsay, I feel you have been distant from the Church and noticed you are no longer wearing garments. Do you mind sharing your religious beliefs? If that's too personal, that's fine. I only want to listen without telling you what to believe. If you are willing, we could talk over dinner, or find a private time to talk with me and Mom." This approach gives Lindsay control over whether she even wants to have the conversation, and it creates parity by making her more equal in the discussion. It also increases containment, since Lindsay can control who takes part (whether the whole family at that moment, or only the parents later). Skills that Dad can apply to strengthen and protect their relationship during the conversation include:

  o **Be genuinely curious.** Dad needs to be open and listen with curiosity and without responding or rebutting so that he can understand why Lindsay's beliefs have changed and what she now believes.

  o **Ask questions.** Dad can use the format "I'd be curious to know . . . " This format works well because it primes Dad to be curious and ensures that he is really asking a question instead of making a rebuttal.

  o **Listen.** Dad needs to make sure he is really listening. This requires making sure Lindsay is talking a lot more than him. Dad could actively think, *I need to let Lindsay talk at least 80% of the time*, and use positive body language (leaning forward, nodding, main-

---

5. David B. Ostler, *Bridges: Ministering to Those Who Question*, 8, 77, 100. Many members who have a faith crisis feel others will reject them because of it. Many members won't initially describe their concerns but will instead evaluate in stages whether it is safe for them to express their feelings. You will need to establish trust before they will fully disclose their reasons and concerns.

taining a relaxed posture, keeping eye contact) to help him be more open and show Lindsay that he truly wants to know.

o **Repeat back key points.** When Lindsay makes a point, Dad can repeat back what he believes the point is. Then Lindsay knows he is listening, and she can correct any misunderstandings.

To establish trust, it is absolutely crucial to avoid being judgmental or argumentative. In a 2017 BYU devotional, President M. Russell Ballard emphasized this point when he recounted being asked, "If I have family or friends who are less active, how far do I go in my attempts to bring them back?" He then told the audience, "My answer is please do not preach to them! Your family members or friends already know the Church's teachings. They don't need another lecture! What they need—what we all need—is love and understanding, not judging."[6]

• **Try to change Lindsay's beliefs.** As we discussed, the effort to change another's beliefs can be moral and effective.[7] As Latter-day Saints, we value agency and know we shouldn't attempt to change people's beliefs through coercion or manipulation. Telling others that they are wrong and offering unwanted advice simply doesn't work. If Lindsay can discuss her beliefs openly and consider her dad's thoughts, she may revise her beliefs. However, given the personal nature of religious beliefs, that openness is only possible if she trusts her dad.

This kind of conversation must start with strengthening the relationship and building trust through learning and listening. Dad needs to make sure Lindsay knows that she can say anything she wants without fear of judgment or rejection, and that she will not be treated as unfaithful or evil. When there is trust, Dad can:

o **Practice cognitive empathy.** Dad could use questions to understand what Lindsay believes and how she arrived at her beliefs. Latter-day Saints may pre-suppose that those who leave the Church do so because they were inconsistent with regular spiritual practices (prayer, scripture study, church attendance, fasting, temple worship, etc.), committed sin that caused them to lose the Spirit, or simply took offense. While these factors may play a role, the primary reasons for leaving the Church are often more

---

6. M. Russell Ballard, "Questions and Answers."

7. See "Change others' opinions and beliefs" in chapter 6.

complex and multifaceted. In *Bridges*, I describe that many leave for completely different reasons.[8]

o **Ask more questions.** Dad could ask questions to assess Lindsay's certainty and help him understand what she is still trying to figure out. He could say, "Lindsay, how certain are you . . . ?" He can follow-up with "Have you always felt that?" If she says no, then he can ask "What has changed?" These questions help Dad not only understand the issue but also how Lindsay's thinking has changed.

o **Assess what would change her mind.** Once Dad understands how and why her beliefs changed, he can then ask, "Can you think of anything that would let you believe in the Church again?" or "Do you feel you could ever come back to Church?" Dad must also be willing to accept the answers that Lindsay gives him, regardless of how painful they might be.

Tips for Religious Discussions

- Build a trusted relationship so others know they can talk openly without judgment or loss of status or relationship.
- Honor agency; listen to understand; don't preach, coerce, or manipulate.
- Don't use language that vilifies those who no longer believe, like apostate, wayward, deceived, or non-believer. All these create out-group bias.
- Find the best setting to create parity, containment, and embodiment.

Respectfully Exploring Someone Else's Opinion

Jack lives in Idaho and is talking on the phone with his friend Amy in Virginia. The conversation wanders, and Jack asks what Amy thinks about President Biden's executive ruling pardoning people convicted of federal crimes for marijuana possession.[9] The conversation broadens to whether marijuana should be legalized.

Jack supports full legalization for both medicinal and recreational use, while Amy favors only legalizing it for medical purposes. As they talk, Jack

---

8. Ostler, *Bridges*, 47–60. Chapter 4, titled "Why People Leave," explains the major reasons why people in a faith crisis leave religion, contrasting these reasons with what is typically assumed: they are lazy, offended, or have committed some sin that caused the Spirit to withdraw.

9. See "Statement from President Biden on Marijuana Reform," The White House.

asks Amy what led her to her opinion. She answers that she has a sister who has been in and out of drug rehab and that she thinks her sister's drug use started with marijuana. Jack responds with his worry about his brother in Idaho who uses marijuana and could be jailed if caught, since possession is a felony in the state.

While Amy thinks recreational marijuana use should be illegal, she also thinks it should only be a misdemeanor. A felony can ruin someone's life and limit their future employment and housing options, which makes little sense to her for non-violent casual marijuana use. Both agree the current system doesn't provide enough resources for addiction. Amy tells Jack that she read about a unique program in Virginia that might help her sister. Jack's mind then gets distracted by a work email he receives, and he asks her to send him the article about it.

They each ask questions to understand the other's experience and opinions. They are genuinely curious about the other's perspectives. Neither dominates the discussion and both remain open and respectful. They support each other in their concerns and fears. When they hang up, they still have different beliefs, but they see new perspectives. So, how did Jack and Amy do?

- **Setting**—How would we rate the setting for this conversation?
    - *Time:* High. The phone call was open-ended, and they could spend the time they wanted to talk.
    - *Attention:* High. Although Jack's mind wandered to what was on his computer, he remained engaged for the rest of the conversation and asked for more information.
    - *Parity:* High. Amy and Jack are friends with neither holding power over the other.
    - *Containment:* High. Nobody else was listening, and they could say whatever they wanted.
    - *Embodiment:* Medium/High. They know each other and can recognize tones, interest, and tension. In-person conversation is always better than ones conducted by telephone, but that was not possible for them.
    - *Consent:* High. Jack and Amy don't need to ask permission for this conversation; it is natural, and either can withdraw if they choose.

- **Objective**—When they started the phone call, they didn't set up an objective except to connect. When marijuana came up, they consciously or unconsciously learned from each other and gained additional understanding. Their opinions changed somewhat, although they still didn't come to complete agreement.

Both parties likely left the conversation feeling connected to each other. The topic is personal and emotional, but they patiently listened and were both open and interested in learning. They aren't experts, but even this conversation made them more interested in the topic and more open when information about marijuana appeared in their news sources.

Summary: How to Learn How Someone Else Thinks

- Ask questions and be curious.
- Practice cognitive empathy, wanting to know *why* they think that, not what they think.
- Acknowledge mistakes and extreme positions on your side.
- Try to listen more than you talk. Hold back if necessary, so you don't dominate.
- Ask what has helped them form their beliefs.

Discussions in the Sphere of Deviance

Sam is talking with his coworker Bill when the 2020 presidential election comes up. Bill believes the election was stolen and has watched a YouTube video claiming an Italian defense contractor uploaded software to a satellite that switched votes from Donald Trump to Joe Biden. This is called ItalyGate,[10] which fits the definition of a conspiracy theory, and Sam doesn't believe it. Sam is angry because he believes that bad actors have falsely claimed that the election was stolen. He believes Donald Trump, and Trump's refusal to accept the outcome of the 2020 election is affecting the stability of democracy in the US.

After asking Bill a few questions, Sam realizes Bill isn't open to changing his opinion. Because Sam doesn't want to damage the relationship nor waste his time talking about Bill's belief, he says, "Bill, I don't agree, and I don't want our work relationship to be affected, so let's talk about something else."

---

10. Reuters Staff, "Fact Check: Evidence Disproves Claims of Italian Conspiracy to Meddle in U.S. Election (Known as #ItalyGate)."

How did Sam do?

- **Setting**—How would we rate the setting for this conversation?
  - o *Time:* Low. In a work setting, there isn't enough time to talk extensively about their very different beliefs.
  - o *Attention:* Medium. Although they are both very interested in the validity of the election, both will likely talk past each other because of their certainty in their beliefs.
  - o *Parity:* High. Bill and Sam are coworkers.
  - o *Containment:* High. Nobody else was listening, and they could say whatever they wanted.
  - o *Embodiment:* High. They know each other and can recognize tones, interest, and tension.
  - o *Consent:* Low. Sam thinks the conversation will potentially damage their relationship.
- **Objective**—Sam recognized that he wasn't going to change Bill's mind. In Sam's mind, Bill's belief was too extreme for reasonable discussion. Sam did a good job of ending the conversation by politely telling Bill that he didn't want to discuss the topic, while acknowledging his different belief.

For Sam, ItalyGate falls into what Mónica Guzmán calls the sphere of deviance, where there is a lack of shared reality. Because there is little common ground, one's objectives in the conversation are limited. Sam chose to avoid the conversation in order to not negatively impact his relationship. Topics that fall into this sphere of deviance are based on one's own perspective, and they vary from person to person. You determine whether a topic is so extreme that there isn't enough common ground to have a meaningful conversation. You can tell the other person you don't want to talk about it. If you do talk about it, then do it with respect, without being condescending.

Getting Together with Friends

Valerie and Jim invite three couples over to their house for games and food. They enjoy catching up on their families, work, and church. Over time, the conversation moves to the latest controversy at school regarding student access to books. Valerie teaches at the local high school and has used books in her class that include queer characters.

Mike thinks some books in the library are too adult for high schoolers. His young son has been talking with his friends and has asked Mike questions about sexuality that he doesn't think his son is old enough to consider. Mike believes that sexuality shouldn't be taught in school and is best taught by parents.

Stephanie feels some political leaders are trying to scare parents with the threat that their child will become transgender by reading these books and becoming aware that transgender people exist. Since Stephanie has a transgender friend, she always wants to defend her friend's rights and societal status.

Danny states his belief in the Proclamation on the Family's teaching that gender is eternal[11] and says that "transgenderism"[12] is part of Satan's plan.

Peter just stays silent. Only his wife knows that he is gay and that theirs is a mixed-orientation marriage.

Pretty soon everyone is talking and wanting to assert their opinions. They interrupt each other as they to get their point of view across. No one gets angry or loud, but it's clear everyone is tense. Peter is vague when asked what he thinks.

Many discussions start out casual but either gradually or suddenly shift to controversial topics. Before we know it, we find ourselves in the middle of an intense, sometimes contentious discussion. The conversation takes on a life of its own with unprepared people who subconsciously react like a herd of elephants.

Let's step back and look at this discussion.

- **Setting**—How was the setting for this conversation?

  o *Time:* High. The conversation occurred during a gathering that still had plenty of time left.

  o *Attention:* Potentially high for those who are interested.

  o *Parity:* Medium. Although all are friends, the large group means that some are more comfortable speaking up than others. Those people may show confidence in a way that gives them more power.[13] Remember that confidence bias leads us to confer more cred-

---

11. "The Family: A Proclamation to the World," The Church of Jesus Christ of Latter-day Saints.

12. *Transgenderism* as a term is often felt to be derogatory and dehumanizing as it reduces transgender people to a condition. See Billie Olsen, "LGBTQ+ Terms to Avoid and What to Use Instead."

13. See "Confidence bias" in chapter 3.

ibility on those who seem more confident, regardless of whether their ideas are actually better.

   o *Containment:* Low. With larger groups it is harder to ensure that what is said does not go beyond the group.

   o *Embodiment:* High. Everyone is physically present.

   o *Consent:* Medium. The conversation evolved and people could participate as they wanted. Stephanie feels strongly and is willing to speak up even though it is uncomfortable. Peter and his wife don't want to talk and, so far, have avoided being cornered and having to give their opinion.

- **Objective**—Since no one is directing the conversation, it has no clear objective. This conversation started out as friends having a casual conversation. It evolved and drifted into a controversial area with potential disagreement.

A challenging or difficult conversation becomes increasingly so with more people involved. While we may not be able to control the group when we find ourselves in the midst of an increasingly or potentially contentious group discussion, there are a couple ways we can help the conversation remain productive and non-contentious:

- **Use our best skills and set the example.** Applying the principles we have learned, we can set a tone for the group by asking questions, probing epistemology, and assessing others' certainty. Use inclusive and in-group language. We don't need to express our own beliefs; if pressed, we can say, "I'm really curious to know what everyone thinks, and I want to give others the opportunity to explain their opinions." We can also choose to not participate at all and excuse ourselves from the conversation to avoid becoming emotionally involved or risking rifts in our relationships.

For Group Conversations

- Set the example. People will often model what you do.
- Be curious and ask questions.
- Avoid out-grouping. Use inclusive language like "us" and "we" whenever possible; try to avoid "them" and "they."
- Admit extremism and the mistakes by people on "your side."

- **Facilitate and organize the group.** Depending on the group situation, we can volunteer to organize the discussion so everyone can take part and talk about an important topic productively. We might politely interrupt the emotions by saying, "This discussion is important, and I would like to try an approach to talk about it without creating contention. Are you up for trying something new? I think it could be interesting and helpful."

  If they consent, suggest this strategy: one person takes about two minutes to say what they think about the topic, then others ask questions, and the first person takes one minute to respond. After three questions, move to the next person. Then someone else can explain their thoughts and answer a few questions. Make sure everyone knows they can participate as they choose and do not have to speak up or ask questions.

  With all in agreement, and a momentary break to calm emotions, we can resume the conversation with: "Okay, who wants to be first? Take about two minutes. If you go long, we'll tell you." After someone says what they think, we can encourage curious understanding by asking, "Okay, who has a question?" Make sure people ask questions to learn and discover. If someone wishes to make a statement instead of asking a question, we can interrupt and say, "That's not a question. Do you want to rephrase that as a question (as if we're on Jeopardy)? Or would you like to go next to tell us what you think—after we are done with questions?"

  This simple technique comes from 3Practices[14] as discussed in chapter 7, where people, including strangers, are taught to talk in this structured way. Since everyone gets to take part equally, it increases parity and promotes listening and curiosity by ensuring that all can contribute without individual voices dominating the conversation. Formalizing what began as a casual conversation may seem awkward at first, but the group will likely appreciate the efforts to positively affect the atmosphere by steering the conversation into something more productive and healthy.

---

14. See the 3Practices website.

<table>
<tr><td colspan="1">Spontaneous Structured Discussion</td></tr>
</table>

• Someone takes about two minutes to make their point.
• Someone else asks a question—a real question, not a statement.
• The first person takes one minute to answer the question.
• After several questions, someone else makes their point in about two minutes.
• And so on.

Interrupting a heated conversation to structure it like this takes bravery. It feels risky, but it can lead to an excellent discussion. People express themselves, ask questions, and learn what others are thinking. It is respectful of others and their opinions, and it can be much better than simply avoiding the discussion or letting it devolve into a contentious argument. Sometimes, one person must jump into the saddle and be the rider when the conversational elephant heads straight into a tangle of brambles.

Politics and Social Issues on Social Media

Sara and Jane are friends on Facebook. Jane thinks of Sara as a casual acquaintance in real life. In the few minutes before Jane's kids come home from school, Jane scrolls through Facebook and sees a post from Sara affirming that "Black Lives Matter." Jane sees her long post and skims through it, absorbing the gist that Sara thinks policing is racist. Jane feels disturbed that the police murdered George Floyd but also frustrated that people seem to elevate Black lives above other lives. She thinks there are a few rotten apples in the police, but she is also concerned by the scale of the BLM demonstrations, some of which have become violent. Since her kids are just about to arrive home from school, she types, "All Lives Matter," feels better, and puts her phone away. She gets a snack ready for her kids.

Let's step back and evaluate what happened. Sara writes a lengthy post about something that is apparently important to her. Without taking the time to fully read what Sara was saying, but being aware of the contemporary issue, Jane responds with a terse statement expressing her disagreement.

Let's evaluate how Jane did:

- **Objective**—Jane believes all people are God's children and we shouldn't discriminate. She thought a simple rebuttal using "All Lives Matter" would be a quick way to help Sara know that highlighting Black lives was discriminatory. Her hope may have been to wake Sara up through this simple message, but the real message she sent was that Sara is wrong. Telling people they are wrong seldom changes minds, creates understanding, or builds a closer relationship.

- Setting—
    o *Time:* Low. Jane only had a few seconds to respond to Sara's long post.
    o *Attention:* Jane's attention is low. She knows the kids will be home soon and only skims Sara's post to get the gist.
    o *Parity:* Medium. It's Sara's Facebook page, and she put her opinions out for all her friends to see. Jane is a casual friend.
    o *Containment:* Low. Sara's friends can see Jane's comments.
    o *Embodiment:* Low. There is no embodiment, facial expressions, or body language.
    o *Consent:* High. Sara's choice to post on Facebook indicates that she agrees to interact and discuss this topic.
- Bias—When Jane saw Sara's post, she subconsciously felt skeptical of what Sara had written. Although she is friends with Sara, noticing that the post was about racism and BLM made her think of Sara as outside of her group, which meant she naturally had out-group bias and subconsciously thought more skeptically about what Jane wrote.
- Other tools—In this setting, with this type of response, Jane is not using any of the tools required to avoid contentious conversations. She didn't show any curiosity, ask questions, jointly consider facts, evaluate epistemology, or practice cognitive empathy. She didn't even listen to Sara's full thoughts by reading her entire post.

Jane could have scrolled by without saying anything, but then she would have missed an important opportunity to positively engage with Sara. Here are two alternative ways Jane could have responded:

- Listen and learn—Jane could have taken advantage of Sara's lengthy post to build understanding or strengthen their relationship. Sara felt strongly enough about the subject to write publicly, knowing some of her friends would disagree. She wanted engagement and was trying to convince readers to think differently. Jane could be curious and say to herself, *I want to hear what Sara is really saying and see where she is coming from.* She could come back to the post, read it clearly, and then post honest, curious questions. After reading Sara's and others' answers, she could even put forward the reasons she feels differently, politely listen, and respond openly.

If Jane wants to do this, she must want to listen, learn, and reflect on her own beliefs. Jane could say "I'd be curious to know . . ." or "Have you always felt this way? If not, what changed?" or "On a scale of 1 to 10 how certain are you that . . ." Jane could also respond in ways that acknowledge mistakes or denounce extremism on her side.

- **Try to change Sara's beliefs**—Social media is a hard place to change minds. The setting is poor, and embodiment is low; we cannot see anybody's body language or infer emotion. Containment is low; everyone can see what we say or write, making exploration and openness difficult. Social media is also a slow and disconnected means of communication. Our comments may go easily unnoticed or forgotten, and responses may be delayed, making it difficult to have the back and forth required for meaningful conversation.

Instead of continuing the discussion on social media, Jane could message Sara and invite her to share hot chocolate at the local café or go for a walk. There, they could discuss their thoughts about what the BLM movement, policing, and the George Floyd murder mean for society. This offer makes it clear that Jane wants to discuss the issue in depth, and if Sara agrees, then they can talk with high levels of time, attention, and parity—since they are meeting on neutral turf, and anyone can leave if they want or change the subject and talk about something else. Containment is good, since they can have relatively private conversations in a café or while walking. Embodiment is high, since they are in person.

Using Social Media

- Keep in mind that social media is a poor setting for meaningful discussions. It has low embodiment and containment.

- Before engaging, clarify your objectives, with the most effective one being to build relationships or to listen and learn. Trying to change someone's mind on social media is difficult and can lead to contention because of its poor setting.

- You can build relationships with people with whom you disagree by affirming without agreeing, using simple comments such as "Thanks for sharing what you believe" or "Glad we can hold our different views while respecting each other."

Before you leave this chapter, think back to recent conversations, evaluate them, and see what you can learn.

Book Group Questions
• See if someone is willing to share a real or imagined scenario like those from this chapter. Have them describe it and analyze what went right and what went wrong.

CHAPTER 9

Practice Makes Perfect

While the Atonement is meant to help us all become more like Christ, it is not meant to make us all the same. Sometimes we confuse differences in personality with sin. We can even make the mistake of thinking that because someone is different from us, it must mean they are not pleasing to God. This line of thinking leads some to believe that the Church wants to create every member from a single mold—that each one should look, feel, think, and behave like every other. This would contradict the genius of God, who created every man different from his brother, every son different from his father. Even identical twins are not identical in their personalities and spiritual identities.

—Elder Dieter F. Uchtdorf[1]

That which we persist in doing becomes easier, not that the task itself has become easier, but that our ability to perform it has improved.

—President Heber J. Grant[2]

This chapter has simple practice exercises that can help us learn helpful principles for having meaningful conversations. By understanding how these principles work in imaginary situations, we can put them to work in our real lives. After all, dancers learn to dance not through reading about dancing or watching YouTube videos, but through trial and error. They take to the dance floor, try some moves, feel the rhythms, and make lots of mistakes. Instructors teach, but dancers must do the work themselves. So while the first steps may feel forced and mechanical, with practice, what initially was klutzy and clumsy becomes natural, beautiful, and automatic. Eventually the dancer never even thinks about the steps as they continue on to more advanced moves. When they dance, their body just knows what to do. It can be the same in our discussions.

Invite a friend to help and practice together. Don't shortchange your learning by skipping these exercises. We only learn by doing. We want these concepts to become natural, like muscle memory, so we don't even think about them. Bookmark or tag these exercises so you can refer to them whenever you find yourself slipping into old habits.

---

1. Dieter F. Uchtdorf, "Four Titles."
2. *Teachings of the Presidents of the Church: Heber J. Grant*, 35. Grant attributed this quote to Ralph Waldo Emerson.

Practice Listening

Next time you have a discussion, practice listening. Listening isn't being silent; it includes asking questions and giving affirming responses to keep the conversation going. Active listening takes real effort to get inside the other person's mind and understand where they are coming from. Ask yourself questions like: *Why is this important to them? What are they seeing that I am not? What caused them to come to this belief?* Notice any tendencies you have to interrupt, correct, or explain away what they are saying. The tendency to interrupt is hard to overcome, but it is disrupting to the person talking. If you notice yourself interrupting, you can say, "Excuse me; please continue." When we apologize when we interrupt, it creates a safer environment for the other person to share. Avoid thinking about ways to refute or argue against their thinking. Make sure you are silent and your discussion partner is talking at least 80 percent of the time. Make it natural and keep the conversation going. Ask yourself whether this is hard or easy for you.

Ask Curious Questions

Find a conversation partner. Let them know you are trying to find better ways to communicate, and you would like to practice your ability to ask curious questions. Pick a topic that they feel comfortable talking about, preferably one where you don't agree (unless you need a warmup topic first). Make sure it is a topic that won't alienate either of you if you find yourselves disagreeing more than expected. Ask them questions so that you know what they believe and why. Examples include:

- I'd be curious to know . . .
- Why is this issue important to you?
- How certain are you that . . . ?
- What has led you to feel that . . . ?
- What sorts of things might change your mind?
- I don't understand; can you clarify?

Try Cognitive Empathy

Do this with the same or a different partner. Tell them you want to practice asking questions to understand how and why someone believes what they do. Pick a belief that won't be alienating; it doesn't need to be something you disagree about. Ask them to state their belief and then ask them questions that help you understand their epistemology (way of knowing) and the experiences that led them to that belief. Here are the questions discussed in chapter 7 that might be helpful:

- Have you always thought . . . ?
- What life experiences have influenced your belief in . . . ?
- How certain are you that . . . ?
- Is there anything that could change your certainty . . . ?

Chapter 7 also discussed five epistemological categories that lead to beliefs: feelings, culture, religious, reason, and evidence.[3] As you hear your partner's answers to the above questions, see whether you can identify which of these categories their beliefs come from. (Remember, beliefs can come from more than one category.) Finally, reflect with your partner on which questions worked and what other questions you could have asked. Repeat this exercise regularly, as cognitive empathy is a powerful and useful skill.

Take the Ideological Turing Test

Find a partner and let them know you want to talk about a belief on which you disagree. It doesn't have to be controversial, but the exercise works better if it is. Let your partner know that you are going to take the Ideological Turing Test by pretending you believe as they do and articulating their position. (You may need to ask questions about their belief to make sure you understand!) Then they tell you how close you got to their thinking. Repeat until your partner says you pass. After you are done, maybe your partner will want to try. You'll likely come away impressed with the power of this tool.

For even more fun, choose a third person to be the audience. You and your conversation partner both take the Ideological Turing Test by advocating for the other person's position on two different topics, then ask the audience member if they can tell who really believes what.

Practice In-grouping

When we talk with people in our group, we feel connection. We naturally extend kindness to them and treat their ideas more forgivingly. But when we see them as being outside our group, we are skeptical and critical.

---

3. See "Use cognitive empathy" in chapter 7.

As you practice in-grouping, you more naturally include people, even if they have different beliefs or come from groups you commonly think of as not your own. Your partner doesn't even need to know you are practicing in-grouping as you talk with them. Try these ideas in your conversation:

- Find some commonality with your discussion partner and use that commonality in your mind to pull them into your group. When nothing is obvious, consider the dignity we should afford them as a fellow human, and try to view them with the love our heavenly parents have.

- Use "we" and "us" to pull people into your group.

- Avoid using "they" or "others" to refer to people who have different beliefs. Instead use neutral terms like, "one who thinks . . ." or "those of us who think differently."

- Eliminate negative terms to refer to those who think differently than you. Eliminate religious labels like "apostates," "deceived," or "enemies." Eliminate political labels that demean like "radicals," "extremists," or any hyper-partisan labels.

Try this variation: explain to your conversation partners how in-groups and out-groups work, which will help them learn this simple principle. Then, together, identify the out-group names and labels you hear in conversations around you. Do this for both religious and political beliefs. Then discuss out-group labels that get applied to you and describe your feelings about these labels. Listen to conversations around you and see whether you can identify common out-group labels. Afterwards, you can privately reflect on how this went. What questions made you feel good and which ones made you feel angry, hurt, or defensive? Consider what you can learn. For extra credit, read or watch your preferred media and see how many out-group labels you can identify.

See Extremism and Mistakes in Your Group

This exercise is best done with a friend who shares similar beliefs. Explain to your friend you are trying to reduce in-group bias and be more critical of the extremism and excesses that is prevalent in your group. Pick a topic on which you both have good agreement. Ask if your friend would join you in critiquing the ways your group is extreme or makes mistakes regarding that issue. To be more effective, you can learn common criticisms the other side has about your group's position. Likewise, you can consider ways your in-group bias causes you to minimize extremism in your group. Discuss those criticisms and evaluate the extent of their validity. This exercise helps you see that for almost every issue, your own side includes an extreme position that you disagree with. When you acknowledge that, you reduce your in-group bias and develop a clearer view of the limitations of your religious, political, or social group.

Ask Questions on Social Media

Social media is one of the hardest places to practice excellent communication skills, but it is also one of the most accessible. When you are on social media and scrolling through posts or tweets, find one where you have a difference of belief and ask a sincere and curious question. Don't ask questions to try to change the other person; instead ask questions to better understand their beliefs. Later, come back and see whether others respond, then ask another question. You need not respond to each one; you get to choose whether the engagement is helpful. If the responses become a distraction, sign off for a while. See how this feels and whether it is a useful approach for you.

Evaluate Your Media

Audit your news media. Start by listing all the news media you used recently. Then use a tool to identify how biased and accurate it is, or just search for "media bias and reliability" and click on links you find interesting.[4] Identify the bias and the reliability of the media that you use. Decide whether to drop or add any media. Even if you make no changes, this exercise will increase your awareness.

Find Common Ground

This is best with a friend who thinks differently. Let's say you have different opinions on abortion. One of you favors laws permitting a woman to make choices about whether to end her pregnancy, the other favors laws restricting abortion except in specific circumstances. You can tell your friend that you are trying to explore common ground, and you know they believe differently about abortion. You would like to find common ground about both women's choice and protecting fetal life. Then spend ten to twenty minutes talking about what you agree on. While you do this, you can practice cognitive empathy and asking questions. Finding common

---

4. See "Find and use reliable information" in chapter 6.

ground doesn't mean compromising your moral values. Even people who are staunchly pro-choice or staunchly pro-life likely agree on the need for better prenatal health care and post-birth family and child support.

Plan Ahead

Before you enter a conversation, use the planning tools to help you think ahead.[5] Ask yourself:

- What do I want from this conversation?
- Is this in the sphere of consensus, legitimate debate, or deviance?
- What is the setting (time, attention, parity, containment, embodiment, and consent)? Will it be appropriate for my goals? Do I want to change anything?
- What information do I have about the topic? Is it reliable?
- Am I emotionally prepared for the topic?

Get Comfortable with Mistakes

Expect to make mistakes, because you will. Our brains are finite and imprecise. We may never master our biases, recognize our limitations, or gain the experience to fully overcome them. We should extend grace to others, as they will make mistakes, too, and we don't want to hold them to a perfect standard that we ourselves cannot achieve. As conflict resolution expert Guy Burgess acknowledges,

> Whenever I do these polarization-related interviews, I always wish I'd said some things differently or feel I missed a vital point, or feel that my suboptimal wording would likely cause some people to misunderstand me. Aside from my own mistakes, the polarized nature of our society means that some people will be filtering any of these discussions through a very pessimistic lens, looking for any small misstep or thing they disagree with as an indicator that the whole concept of depolarization is faulty and oblivious.[6]

Furthermore, do not expect that your conversation will always reach some conclusion. Our brains want closure; when we find it, we get a dose of hormones that make us feel good, but our conversations often continue without people coming to an agreement, so resist the urge to decide that

5. See chapter 7, "Tools to use in conversations."
6. Guy Burgess, "Is Liberal Bias Impeding U.S. depolarization and conflict resolution efforts?"

the conversation is complete. Instead, in your mind, and perhaps in your partner's mind, set an expectation that you want to continue to discuss.

Don't Move On Yet!

- Don't read past these exercises too quickly.
- Do something—bookmark this section, talk to a friend or family member, set a date, or try something now, so you don't forget what you have learned.

Earlier we compared the give-and-take of a conversation with dancing. Well-practiced and skilled dancers execute an almost perfect dance almost every time. They learn the routines and master the steps. It's not that way in conversations. We will always make mistakes and regret something we said or think of a way we could have done it better. It's the way conversations are—full of mistakes and the humanness we share with others. When you make mistakes, acknowledge them, apologize, and try to learn. Extend grace to yourself and to others.

Each mistake is an opportunity to learn. Don't beat yourself up over the mistakes you make. With practice, you will get more comfortable and make fewer mistakes in the future. Unlike the dancer, you won't ever get to where you think you have mastered it. You will conversationally step on toes, miss cues, and get out of rhythm. But that's okay. Don't let it stop you from having these important and essential conversations.

Book Group Questions

- Try the Ideological Turing Test outlined in this chapter, with the whole book group as the audience, as you and your conversation partner advocate for each other's position about two different topics. Then see if the audience can tell who really believes what.
- Did you try any of the other practices? Which ones? What happened?
- Does anyone want to try them together at another time?

CHAPTER 10

Visions

Individually and as a people we can and should be a people of peace and reconciliation. I consider this as one of our prime responsibilities toward our children and their children. . . . It takes empathy and action to influence the future of mankind based on dignity, honesty, and eternal values.

—Elder Dieter F. Uchtdorf[1]

Societies become strong when they . . . see relationships in terms not of interests but of moral commitment. . . . The concept of covenant . . . changes everything it touches, from marriage to friendship to economics and politics, by turning self-interested individuals into a community in pursuit of the common good.

—Rabbi Jonathan Sacks[2]

We can only change our human condition if there is a change in our individual makeup and outlooks as well as our soul and mind.

—The Qur'an, as quoted by Alwi Shahbi[3]

What is God thinking about our society right now? Is He pleased with the acrimony we have in public life? Does He smile when He sees family members unable to talk with each other because of perceived irreconcilably different beliefs? Or does He grieve and repeat His words to Enoch?

Behold these thy brethren; they are the workmanship of mine own hands, and I gave unto them their knowledge, in the day I created them; and in the Garden of Eden, gave I unto man his agency; And unto thy brethren have I said, and also given commandment, that they should love one another, and that they should choose me, their Father; but behold, they are without affection, and they hate their own blood. (Moses 7:32–33)

Does God weep today (Moses 7:28)?

1. Marianne Holman Prescott, "Seek and Speak Out for Peace, Elder Uchtdorf Urges During Volkstrauertag Service." Elder Uchtdorf gave these remarks on Volkstrauertag, which is the people's day of mourning in Germany, commemorating all who died in armed conflicts. It was first observed in 1952 and later broadened to include those who died due to oppressive government.

2. Jonathan Sacks, *Morality*, 375.

3. Alwi Shihab, "Building Bridges to Harmony Through Understanding."

Two years ago, I sat on a beach with a family member I hadn't seen for a few years. We watched the surf, caught some rays, and chatted. Our conversation turned to the concerns we had about our families and communities, and the challenges we saw with our fellow Church members. He expressed his concern that Latter-day Saints are becoming just like the world, polarized and contentious. He said that at night on his knees, he apologizes to God for the contention and division we have and pleads with God to give us more time to sort out our problems and find the unity that we as Latter-day Saints should have. Ultimate unity and societal harmony won't come until the Savior's return, but if we had more time to show God that we could live in harmony, like my family member prayed, what could we do?

Ponder as You Read

- In what ways can you help the world be less contentious? Do you want to be involved?

- What common ground can you have with others without giving up your values and what is important to you?

- Do we just need to live better individually, or is there a collective work too? If so, how do we get started?

The Common Good

Communal harmony requires us to sacrifice individually for the collective good. Rabbi Sacks calls this *morality*, which he defines as "a concern for the welfare of others, an active commitment to justice and compassion, a willingness to ask not just what is good for me but what is good for *all of us together*. It is about *Us*, not *Me*; about *We*, not *I*."[4] In such a society, we think about the collective good and subordinate personal interests because it is what society needs. While we don't hold our goods and possessions in common, we hold other people's needs and interests in our hearts.

Within Communities of Faith

God has always guided his people towards this concept of *We* and *Us*. Examples include the city of Enoch, the people of Alma, the primitive church after Jesus's resurrection, Fourth Nephi, and the early days of

---

4. Sacks, 17; emphasis added.

the Restoration.[5] Discipleship has always included concern for others and taking care of their needs. Today, Latter-day Saints don't practice the law of consecration in the same way that early Church members were asked to do, but as a part of temple covenants, echoed in the *Handbook*, we promise to "keep the law of consecration, which means that members dedicate their time, talents, and everything with which the Lord has blessed them to building up Jesus Christ's Church on earth."[6] We give our whole hearts and souls for Zion. Perhaps some have achieved this fully dedicated discipleship, but most of us are still a work in progress, with hearts and minds aspiring to this level of commitment.

Our Responsibility to Others

This level of communal devotion isn't limited to those who have made similar commitments (i.e. other members of the Church or members of our in-group). Jesus didn't say we only need to love those who belong to our church or our preferred political party, or only those who think like us. We are the Samaritan who is asked to see everyone as our neighbors. Our discipleship includes understanding and ministering to others according

---

5. During the time of Enoch, "the Lord called his people Zion, because they were of one heart and one mind, and dwelt in righteousness; and there was no poor among them" (Moses 7:18). At the Waters of Mormon, Alma "commanded them that there should be no contention one with another, but that they should look forward with one eye, having one faith and one baptism, having their hearts knit together in unity and in love one towards another" (Mosiah 18:21). In Jerusalem shortly following the Savior's resurrection, "all that believed were together, and had all things common; And sold their possessions and goods, and parted them to all men, as every man had need" (Acts 2:44–45). In the time of Fourth Nephi, "there were no contentions and disputations among them, and every man did deal justly one with another" (4 Ne. 1:2). Moroni teaches, "After they had been received unto baptism . . . they were numbered among the people of the church of Christ; and their names were taken, that they might be remembered and nourished . . . And the church did meet together oft, to fast and to pray and to speak one with another concerning the welfare of their souls" (Moro. 6:4–5). In 1831, barely ten months after Joseph Smith organized the Church, he received a revelation outlining our communal responsibilities, including members consecrating their excess properties to the Church for the common good (D&C 42:30–39).

6. "Temple Ordinances for the Living," General Handbook: Serving in The Church of Jesus Christ of Latter-day Saints, 27.2.

to their needs and wants.[7] Our work isn't limited to lifting individuals; we are called to lift entire communities in similar ways. It includes creating a society that reflects God's goodness and meets others' needs, even when their religious beliefs and values are different from our own.

Our doctrine teaches the value of working with others in our communities. We learn from others' different experiences and beliefs and find ways to peacefully live together. Reflecting on this truth, the Church teaches:

> We find meaning in human connection when we climb out of ourselves and discover the dignity of others, even if we disagree. And no one should have to give up their identities. . . . Since no particular group has a monopoly on all that is wise, beautiful and just, everyone can learn from everyone else. Our experiences have gaps that need to be bridged, and our perspectives have blind spots that need to be filled. . . . This engagement between differences is called pluralism, a society organized under common laws and civilization but with no single belief system that wields total influence. Not just one, or even two, but many perspectives and traditions can co-exist within a shared moral framework.[8]

Extending this same level of concern and commitment to those outside of our religious community is harder. Some wonder whether it is really required. Still others wonder whether it is even right at all to interact with those who have different values and beliefs. They may worry that by doing so they aren't defending the faith, or they may feel unfaithful or disloyal hearing people express beliefs that aren't consistent with Latter-day Saint beliefs. Pushing back against these fears, Elder Ulisses Soares emphasizes:

> Societies flourish when both law and culture recognize, respect, and protect the value of each person. The many religious and cultural differences across the globe only enhance that dignity. . . . Our differences are often used as barriers to divide us, when they are actually an opportunity to enrich our

---

7. King Benjamin explains that our responsibility to others includes our understanding their spiritual and temporal wants. He says, "For the sake of retaining a remission of your sins from day to day, that ye may walk guiltless before God—I would that ye should impart of your substance to the poor, every man according to that which he hath, such as feeding the hungry, clothing the naked, visiting the sick and administering to their relief, both spiritually and temporally, according to their *wants*" (Mosiah 4:26; emphasis added). Alma followed this counsel as he led the Church: "They did walk uprightly before God, imparting to one another both temporally and spiritually according to *their needs and their wants*" (Mosiah 18:29; emphasis added).

8. "Difference and Dignity," Newsroom.

lives. Dignity is a moral obligation we feel toward people. . . . Everyone wants to be known, seen and heard.[9]

Dignity and respect should guide our discussions and our aspirations for our communities. In 2018, the Church joined other religious leaders, government officials, and scholars in signing the "Punta del Este Declaration on Human Dignity for Everyone Everywhere," which outlines basic principles to protect individual dignity and elevate humanity. Below are a few points from this declaration illustrating our responsibilities for others:

> Dignity is a status shared by every human being, and the emphasis on everyone and everywhere makes it clear that rights are characterized by reciprocity and involve corresponding duties. Everyone should be concerned not only with his or her own dignity and rights but with the dignity and rights of every human being. Nonetheless, human dignity is not diminished on the ground that persons are not fulfilling their responsibilities to the state and others. . . .
>
> Focusing on human dignity for everyone everywhere encourages people to search for ways to find common ground regarding competing claims and to move beyond exclusively legal mechanisms for harmonizing, implementing, and mutually vindicating human rights and finding solutions to conflicts.[10]

In 2015, the Church illustrated how this works as it acted with other groups in a pluralistic way. Let's take a closer look.

The Utah Compromise

How society chooses to include and extend rights to LGBTQ people has been a contentious societal challenge. Queer[11] people have suffered discrimination, marginalization, and violence. Since it is a minority group, folks outside of it often do not fully understand the level of discrimination, marginalization, and violence that queer people have experienced. A recent *Deseret News* opinion said as much: "People fail to appreciate the

---

9. Ulisses Soares, "Foundations and Fruits of Religious Freedom."

10. "Punta del Este Declaration on Human Dignity for Everyone Everywhere: Seventy Years after the Universal Declaration of Human Rights."

11. Originally a slur, the word "queer" has been embraced by some members of the LGBTQ community. Author Blaire Ostler explains her positive use of the inclusive umbrella term "queer" in her book *Queer Mormon Theology: An Introduction*, 8–10.

brutal history of the basic human rights of marginalized groups, such as gays and lesbians."[12]

In their marginalization, queer people want full rights and respect. At the same time, religious teachings about the morality of sexuality and gender lead churches and individuals to worry that as more Americans support queer rights, a societal majority would force them to change their religious doctrine and practices. They feel that any changes should come from God, not social pressure or shifting majority opinions.[13] These differences seem intractable.

In the mid-2000s, against this backdrop, Troy Williams was executive director of Equality Utah, an LGBTQ advocacy group. A gay man and a former Latter-day Saint, Williams was working to protect queer individuals from housing and employment discrimination. At that time, it was legal for landlords to refuse to rent to queer individuals and for employers to refuse to hire qualified candidates simply because they were LGBTQ. At the same time, religious organizations, including the Church, were concerned that future anti-discriminatory laws might require them to violate their religious beliefs.

Over half a decade, Williams and other leaders from the queer community met regularly with political, religious, and business leaders to find common ground on these issues. They got to know each other personally and learned about each other's needs and concerns. This group developed the Utah Compromise, which was a set of proposals to prohibit employment and housing discrimination based on sexual orientation or gender identity and to provide exemptions to religious organizations. In 2015, the Utah Legislature passed these proposals, and then Governor Gary Herbert signed these proposals into law.

Political, religious, and business leaders praised the Utah Compromise. One leader described it as "something novel and great that people outside of Utah would never imagine that our state would lead in."[14] Herbert said, "I've learned in my years of working with Troy Williams that we get much

---

12. "Legislation should not polarize religious liberties, anti-discrimination protections," *Deseret News*.

13. For example, the Latter-day Saint 11th Article of Faith states: "We claim the privilege of worshiping Almighty God according to the dictates of our own conscience, and allow all men the same privilege, let them worship how, where, or what they may."

14. Carolyn Campbell, "Creating Common Ground: The Uncanny Ability of Activist Troy Williams."

better results and outcomes when we listen with mutual respect, don't blame, and find common ground. This commonality allows us to find mutually beneficial solutions." [15]

Ask Yourself

- How do you think the participants in the Utah Compromise established trust?
- What concerns would you have if you had taken part in a group like this?
- Do you think the Church compromised its values by supporting the Utah Compromise?

Accommodation versus Winner-Takes-All

Today, we have choices humans haven't usually had. It's easy to forget that over thousands of years of human history, regular people seldom had any say in society's organization or the laws and regulations that controlled them. Today, dictators, royalty, or religious leaders rule fewer countries compared to centuries ago. Despite today's continued tragic conflicts, Harvard researcher Steven Pinker concludes that "this may be the most peaceable time in our species's existence."[16] The governments of the most stable, peaceful, and prosperous countries use the voice of the people in some way. When governments listen to the needs and wants of all their citizens, and incorporate them into public policy, they make better decisions and decrease polarization and contention.

In today's polarized American society, however, the democratic ideal is becoming increasingly hijacked by those who are so certain in their beliefs that they can only visualize a society that forces those beliefs (and their associated behaviors) upon others. Thus, it seems that when Republicans are in charge, we go one direction; then, when the Democrats are in charge, we go a completely different direction. Most legislative votes are winner-takes-all, with little crossover from the minority political party. Today, a political mandate for change only requires a narrow margin in a single election. The winner gets to appoint judges, determine legislation, and work to remake society in their image. This is a large part of the alienation that many Americans feel toward the political process.

---

15. Campbell, "Creating Common Ground."
16. Gareth Cook, "History and the Decline of Human Violence."

President Dallin H. Oaks warns us about today's winner-takes-all political environment and calls on us to live together and accommodate others while we protect our rights to believe as we choose. He says:

> I am, therefore, distressed at the way we are handling the national issues that divide us. We have always had to work through serious political conflicts, but today too many approach that task as if their preferred outcome must entirely prevail over all others, even in our pluralistic society. We need to work for a better way—a way to resolve differences without compromising core values. We need to live together in peace and mutual respect, within our defined constitutional rights.[17]

President Oaks highlights the importance of listening and finding ways to accept those who are different. He says, "As a practical basis for co-existence, we should accept the reality that we are fellow citizens who need each other. This requires us to accept some laws we dislike, and to live peacefully with some persons whose values differ from our own. Amid such inevitable differences, we should make every effort to understand the experiences and concerns of others, especially when they differ from our own."[18]

Covenantal Pluralism

Other groups are working for this kind of society. One approach is called *covenantal pluralism,* which actively supports discussion of human rights and responsibilities through engagement, respect, and protection of others, without conceding one's beliefs.[19] Rabbi Irving Greenberg conceived of it as a way for him, as a Jew, to collaborate with Christians, whom he blamed for the Holocaust. Foundational is his belief that "all humans are created in the image of God and endowed by their creator with certain inalienable dignities, among which are infinite value, equality and uniqueness. . . [and] are constantly developing and in the process of learning."[20] Using this model, Greenberg suggests we can solve many societal problems through collaboration, which begins with understanding people, their divinity, and their sincere beliefs and needs.

---

17. Dallin H. Oaks, "Going Forward with Religious Freedom and Nondiscrimination."

18. Oaks, "Going Forward."

19. See W. Christopher Stewart, Chris Seiple, and Dennis R. Hoover, "Toward a Global Covenant of Peaceable Neighborhood: Introducing the Philosophy of Covenantal Pluralism," 1–17.

20. Irving Greenberg, "Covenantal Pluralism," 427.

Templeton Religion Trust,[21] a charity focusing on enriching conversations about today's issues through religious values, uses Greenberg's work in their Covenantal Pluralism Initiative.[22] They use the word *covenantal* to define the obligations of the group to each other, in which they effectively promise to understand the needs and viewpoints of others and include them in the formulation of solutions; it implies a mutual and interested commitment, not just a contractual and transactional way to engage. As Latter-day Saints, we also use the term *covenant* as a sacred promise to God to live life according to certain rules and principles.

The term *pluralism* is used to acknowledge our need for multiple groups to coexist. Diana Eck, who heads The Pluralism Project, defines pluralism thus: "First, pluralism is not diversity alone, but the energetic engagement with diversity. Second, pluralism is not just tolerance, but the active seeking of understanding across lines of difference. Third, pluralism is not relativism, but the encounter of commitments. Fourth, pluralism is based on dialogue."[23] Sharing this principle of pluralism, the Church teaches that "such an ideal works only when people develop the habits and manners of civility in understanding the unique worldviews of their neighbors."[24] Using civility and dignity in our engagement is essential for a pluralistic society and our need to find common ground for complex societal problems.

Greg Bourne, an international conflict resolution expert, describes how our commitment to respect and understanding is essential to finding solutions that work for all of us. He says:

> We are not always going to see eye-to-eye or agree on the solutions to specific issues or concerns. But when we do not agree, there must be an effort to understand the other, identify what we have in common, identify what is the common good, and work respectfully through our differences towards a solution that can be imagined by all.
>
> As we work through areas of disagreement, we do so from the starting point that there is a mutual concern for one another—if for no other reason

---

21. See the Templeton Religion Trust website. Their Areas of Focus page describes covenantal pluralism and asks the question, "How can we transform religious diversity from a troublesome fact we're stuck with and simply have to learn to tolerate into a positive asset?"

22. "Moving from Tolerance to Pluralism," Templeton Religion Trust.

23. "About," The Pluralism Project at Harvard University.

24. "Difference and Dignity," Newsroom.

that the alternative will most certainly erode our social contract with one another, and the health of our society.

What values, then, must we consider? Start with the many values to which most aspire. To be respected. To be heard. To be given a fair chance. Simply said, supported in some form by nearly every religious tradition, to treat others as we wish to be treated. Compassion, empathy, understanding, forgiveness, some degree of grace and yes, dare we say, love—a word we typically shy away from in the public square.

We must choose the better path—and the first step begins with each of us making that choice.[25]

Society is richer when we both share our individual needs and differences and explore them together. In this process, we learn about others, open our minds, and find shared solutions. We are bound to each other and our mutual needs, and we magnify the covenants we have made to God and those around us to love and care for each other.

Being True To Our Values

In our efforts to find common ground, we do not need to give up our values or beliefs. In all these examples, *covenantal* engagement means finding common ground that honors everyone's different values, including our own. We respect what people believe is right and wrong and do not require them to change their moral beliefs to find compromise. This is not a winner-takes-all approach that disregards the validity of the moral beliefs of others, nor is it a relativistic approach that avoids any judgment and requires acceptance of all beliefs. Such relativism is a lazy and condescending form of tolerance that assumes society is better without debate about right and wrong. While tolerance is often thought of as the recognition of differences and the accommodation of everyone, regardless of the validity of their views, in this setting, there is no tension around differences of belief, and therefore there is less ability to examine goodness and to grow individually and collectively.

When people with religious or morally based beliefs gather together and challenge each other's thinking about what is best for society, we are enriched. Sir John Templeton, founder of the Templeton Religion Trust, says,

Tolerance may be a divine virtue, but it could also become a vehicle for apathy. Millions of people are thoroughly tolerant toward diverse religions, but rarely do such people go down in history as creators, benefactors, or leaders

---

25. Greg Bourne, "What Do the Times Require?"

of progress . . . Should we not desire to have our neighbour share insights and try to convey to us the brilliant light that has transformed his life—the fire in his soul? Why settle for a least-common-denominator type of religion based on tolerance alone? More than tolerance, we need constructive competition. When persons on fire for a great gospel compete lovingly to give their finest treasures to each other, will not everyone benefit?[26]

If we can overcome our tendencies toward contention in the arena of value-based discussions, we learn and grow.

Reflect

- What reservations do you have about considering the needs and beliefs of other people?
- Do you give up your integrity by having these discussions with others?
- What do you think about a "constructive and loving competition . . . to give others their finest treasures," as Sir Templeton said?

As Latter-day Saints, we interact with people who are different than ourselves in our church worship and callings. Our congregations are determined by geographic boundaries, not by economic, political, affinity, or generational groupings. At church, we love and serve with people who have different worldviews, different lives, and different needs. We learn from each other as we discuss the gospel and serve each other. Today, I am concerned that controversial issues have created polarization even among and between Latter-day Saints. Without the skills to discuss our differences, we instead avoid meaningful discussions and eliminate opportunities to learn from each other's differences.

If we can discuss conflicting beliefs without contention, we learn and grow. President Oaks gives an example of how he experienced this by listening. He says he has "come to understand better the distress of [LGBTQ] persons who feel that others . . . deny or challenge . . . their access to basic constitutional rights."[27] Through this kind of engagement, we become more thoughtful and better people, and we work together to move our society closer to the Zion we all desire.

While the process of societal accommodation doesn't require us to compromise our values, it does require sacrifice; as Rabbi Sacks says, we

---

26. John Templeton, *Possibility for Over One Hundredfold More Spiritual Information: The Humble Approach in Theology and Science*, 122–123.

27. Oaks, "Going Forward."

sacrifice parts of the "me" for the "us." We subordinate some of our personal needs and wants because it is practically and morally good for us as a collective. President Oaks describes this kind of sacrifice when he says, "Seeking harmony by finding practical solutions to our differences, with love and respect for all people—does not require any compromise of core principles. *This requires us to accept some laws we dislike, and to live peacefully with some persons whose values differ from our own.*"[28]

Some may think this means we should soften how we speak about our values. It doesn't. These settings require us to uphold our values and concerns while we actively listen to understand those of others. We should ardently hold to and advocate for our principles. At times this may mean that there simply isn't common ground to build a productive discussion upon. For example, I can see no common ground with someone who wants to re-segregate society or diminish the rights and opportunities of women. Nor could I find accommodation that would require me to compromise the right to religion and individual worship. My values include the sacredness of human dignity, which prevents me from agreeing to any solution that subjugates or discriminates against certain essential human rights for anyone anywhere. If compromise on these values is expected, I will hold fast and continue to advocate for what I believe. However, as I advocate for my beliefs, I will do so with civility, recognizing the dignity of others.

Possible Futures

In the past, religious institutions have been central to the establishment of societal values, morals, and norms. Capitalism, politics, and even disinterested tolerance cannot provide the creative conflict necessary for value-based engagement. Worried about this decline of societal cohesiveness, Rabbi Sacks describes his concern about the future of democracy and freedom:

> Liberal democracy is at risk. . . . We are not machines, we are people, and people survive by caring for one another. . . . Market economics and liberal politics will fail if they are not undergirded by a moral sense that puts our shared humanity first. Economic inequalities will grow. Politics will continue to disappoint our expectations. There will be a rising tide of anger and resentment, and that, historically, is a danger signal for the future of freedom.[29]

---

28. Oaks, "Going Forward"; emphasis added.
29. Sacks, *Morality*, 17.

With many people leaving organized religion,[30] it is unclear where the creative tension between people with different moral beliefs will emerge. It's unfair and inaccurate to say non-religious people do not have moral and spiritual values and that only organized religion can offer the structured opportunities to gather in our diversity and find commonality. Future societies may have to find other ways to teach and establish these values.

As Latter-day Saints, we can provide at least some of this creative power. Although we are a small minority in America, we have distinctive values and the expansive view that we are all God's children. We are well-organized and have prophetic leaders who proclaim the benefits of societal engagement. We find those values embodied in the humanitarian work the Church does in partnership with other organizations throughout the world.[31]

But the vision of what we could accomplish doesn't lie in some new Church program. Instead, it lies within the individual initiatives we take in our own circles. President Nelson says, "How we treat each other really matters. How we speak to and about others at home, at church, at work, and online really matters. . . . We can literally change the world one person and one interaction at a time. How? By modeling honest differences of opinion with mutual respect and dignified dialogue."[32] This is what we must do in our families and communities. Imagine if, instead of disrupting school boards and marching in the streets, we followed President Nelson's counsel and sat down respectfully with other people, used our best skills, immersed ourselves in others' concerns, expressed our own, and accommodated all those perspectives into the best collective good. (There is a time and a place for marching and disrupting meetings, but often, more progress occurs without contention through skilled conversation.)

30. "Modeling the Future of Religion in America, How U.S. Religious Composition Has Changed in Recent Decades," Pew Research Center. If present trends continue, a majority of Americans will likely identify as belonging to no particular religion by 2070. See "Modeling the Future of Religion in America, If Recent Trends in Religious Switching Continue, Christians Could Make up Less than Half of the U.S. Population Within a Few Decades," Pew Research Center.

31. The Church regularly partners with other organizations for humanitarian assistance. According to their 2021 Annual Report, Latter-day Saints Charities (the humanitarian arm of the Church) donated and assisted 3,909 humanitarian projects in 188 countries, a large share working with diverse religious and non-profit organizations. See "The 2022 Report on How the Church of Jesus Christ Cared for Those in Need," Newsroom.

32. Russell M. Nelson, "Peacemakers Needed."

We must reject winner-takes-all approaches and the false out-grouping assumption that no common ground can be found with those who believe differently. We must also reject the notion that we inherently compromise our beliefs if we accommodate others' needs and perspectives. Jesus set the example as he rejected the criticism of others by dining and interacting with publicans, sinners, Samaritans, those affected by leprosy, and others deemed not worthy of interaction.[33] In these settings, he learned of their needs and concerns and ministered to them.

None of this is easy, and change doesn't happen in a single conversation. As Latter-day Saints, we sometimes receive disrespect because some of our doctrines and principles differ from society at large. However, we are not alone; this happens whenever people interact with others who have different worldviews and beliefs. As the Franciscan priest Richard Rohr acknowledges, these efforts to improve our conversations, relationships, and society do not come easy: "We dedicate our lives to building bridges and paying the price in our bodies for this ministry of reconciliation. The price is that we will always, like all bridges, be walked on from both sides."[34] Bridge-building is worth it. It takes time, sometimes years, with all our patience and love, and all the skills we can sharpen through books like this one. Others may not reciprocate our commitment, but through shared love and respect for each other, we can create a stronger society, built around the needs and desires of more of us.

Book Group Questions

- What do you think about the principles of communal covenants and dignity? What are their strengths and weaknesses?

- What do you think about the Utah Compromise? What challenges would you face if you tried to apply a similar decision-making process in your community, on that topic or on any other?

- Have you ever been involved in community-based problem solving? How did it go? Do you observe principles that would have been helpful?

---

33. One such example among many is Matthew 9:10–11.
34. Richard Rohr, "Following Jesus' Way."

Press Forward, Saints

Friendship is one of the grand fundamental principles of Mormonism to revolutionize and civilize the world, and cause wars and contentions to cease and men to become friends and brothers.

—Joseph Smith[1]

We can't imagine leaving our children and grandchildren the much darker, more dangerous, and less prosperous future that we are currently heading towards.

—Dr. Heidi and Dr. Guy Burgess[2]

Reasons to be Hopeful

At times it may seem that the growing division, conflict, and contempt in the world is just too much to overcome, but I remain hopeful and optimistic. Even with all our internal physical limitations and natural biases, and the external influences and bad actors, God still created us in His own image. We have agency and we can rise above today's challenges to make a better world. Others need not believe in God to join us, for as Elder Dieter F. Uchtdorf says, "the Light of Christ enlightens and saturates the souls of all who hearken to the voice of the Spirit."[3]

As humans, we continually make progress while sometimes sliding backwards. When we measure progress in generations and centuries, we realize that we have made significant steps forward. In the United States, while hunger and food insecurity are persistent problems for many, starvation is largely a thing of the past, few young children work in dark factories or coal mines, chattel slavery (the buying and selling of people as property) is illegal,[4] and women have attained rights and privileges (such as voting and property ownership) that had eluded so many for centu-

---

1. Joseph Smith History, 1838–1856, volume E-1, created 1 July 1843–30 April 1844, p. 1680.

2. Heidi and Guy Burgess, "Fighting Hyper-Polarization for Our Children and Grandchildren—Newsletter 61."

3. Dieter F. Uchtdorf, "Bearers of Heavenly Light."

4. Although illegal in the US, an estimated 40.3 million people worldwide live in some form of slavery today. See the 2018 Global Slavery Index at https://www.globalslaveryindex.org/2018/findings/global-findings/.

ries or millennia. Instead of being ruled by kings and dictators, ordinary people often decide the course of our communities. While some of these changes unfortunately came through violence (the Civil War being a horrendous example), most were achieved through individuals and groups discussing conflicting ideas and peaceably working toward solutions.

Even with the increased contention we feel in today's politics, the challenges of social media, and other polarizing forces, we still continue to naturally learn and improve. In doing so we see glimpses of "things as they really are" (Jacob 4:13) and "put away childish things" (1 Cor. 13:11). Even when we cannot discuss them directly, most of us are listening to and are affected by opposing points of view. Psychologists Hugo Mercier, Dan Sperber, and Tom Stafford suggest that even taking part in social media results in change and moderation:

> The filter bubble is a temporary nuisance, and quite permeable. Sure, the internet makes it easier to form groups around our biased and lazy reasoning; but it also exposes us to the arguments of those outside of our groups. Spend enough time in places like Reddit or Twitter or Facebook, with all the arguing and all the bad ideas fighting one another, and even if you remain silent, someone will voice something that resembles your private opinion, and someone will argue with them. Even as spectators, we can realize when the weaknesses of our justifications have been exposed.[5]

Despite social media's inherent challenges and dangerous pitfalls, the avenues of communication they create can still result in expanded thinking and new perspectives. It happens even more effectively in direct conversations. Good ideas eventually shine through, and we make progress.

If Not Us, Then Who?

Nothing gets better until enough of us decide we want to make it so. We can hope politicians wake up and realize political polarization is one of the major causes for the tearing of our societal fabric, but until then *we* must be the needed change. As Dr. Seuss says, "Unless someone like you cares a whole awful lot, nothing is going to get better. It's not."[6]

Where do we begin?

---

5. David McRaney, *How Minds Change: The Surprising Science of Belief, Opinion, and Persuasion*, 199–200.

6. Theodor Seuss Geisel (Dr. Seuss), *The Lorax*.

Ourselves

Let's start with ourselves individually. While some may have the skills, charisma, and means to organize and influence hundreds or even thousands of people, for most of us our direct impact will be limited to only ourselves and a few close associates. That's all we can do, and maybe it will be just the tipping point to make a global difference. As Robert F. Kennedy emphasized, "Each time a man stands up for an ideal, or acts to improve the lot of others, or strikes out against injustice, he sends forth a tiny ripple of hope, and crossing each other from a million different centers of energy and daring those ripples build a current which can sweep down the mightiest walls of oppression and resistance."[7] Even if our efforts do not make a difference in overall society, they can make us and those around us better and happier.

Recognizing this, some reasonable goals we can set are to:

- Strengthen our skills.
- Resolve to be a better listener.
- Give up language that out-groups and vilifies.
- Choose to engage in hard conversations.
- Make a commitment to understand others.
- Find others, especially in our families, who will join us.

We can make a difference with these modest goals, and that difference can be expanded as we include others in these efforts. As conflict resolution experts tell us, "Everybody complains about hyperpolarization but nowhere near enough people are actually doing something about it. It is critical to replace the current dominant us-vs-them frame with a 'we' frame whereby we all work together to reverse the dynamics that are driving us apart."[8]

Our Families

We all have worldviews that are influenced by the culture and world we live in, and these worldviews are first formulated in the family environments we grow up in. Because of this, parents and other role models are

---

7. Robert F. Kenney, "Day of Affirmation Address."

8. Guy Burgess, Heidi Burgess, Sanda Kaufman, "Applying Conflict Resolution Insights to the Hyper-polarized, Society-wide Conflicts Threatening Liberal Democracies," 357.

best suited to shape the worldview of children and to help them develop immunity to today's destructive forces, giving them skills to avoid getting sucked into today's polarization. The best thing parents can do is be an example. In a 2006 general conference address, Young Women General President Susan W. Tanner warned us to be vigilant in our homes: "Homes are also private places, so unfortunately, we often let down. In our homes and with our families we sometimes become our worst selves with the people who matter the most in our lives."[9] Our children watch us and learn from our words and actions. To teach our children, we can discuss the questions and exercises in this book around the dinner table, teach specific lessons about these principles, or possibly incorporate them into *Come Follow Me.*[10] Basic skills that can help children avoid contention and polarization, increase learning, and strengthen relationships include:

- Developing curiosity.
- Learning to listen.
- Developing skills to ask questions.
- Discerning bias and reliability.
- Understanding how to analyze critically.
- Learning how to see challenges in the world without becoming cynical.
- Being courageous enough to disagree while being agreeable.
- Avoiding labeling and out-grouping.

These, of course, need to be adapted to our children's ages. A "Resource Guide" at the end of the book contains specific materials for teaching children.

Consider
• Which family members or friends can you ask to join you in preventing contention and healing divisions?
• What conversations do you need to have with those in your close circle to bring respect, accommodation, and greater peace?

9. Susan W. Tanner, "I Am the Light Which Ye Shall Hold Up."

10. *Come Follow Me—For Individuals and Families* is a program developed by The Church of Jesus Christ of Latter-day Saints. Families and individuals can use these materials for daily scripture study. It also constitutes the curriculum for Church-based Sunday School and Primary class instruction.

Our In-groups

Because in-grouping and out-grouping contribute to bias and contention, members of our own group are more sympathetic to our efforts and see them more favorably. Thus, outside our family, we are most effective at stopping polarization and division with those who share our political or religious beliefs. According to Zach Elwood, a conflict resolution expert, "we can only influence people who are similar to us; our righteous judgments of the other side and desires that they improve themselves have no real influence on them. Research shows change of a group must come from within, so we need more people, both conservatives and liberals, thinking about these things and thinking about how they can make their own political groups less toxic."[11] The same can be said for any kind of group.

Our groups may have shared religious or political beliefs, or they may be our neighbors who know us well and trust our sincerity. In-group conversations can happen through social media and informal gatherings or in settings we create. The practice exercises in chapter 9 and the questions at the end of each chapter are well-suited for book groups, and the "Ideas for Book Groups" at the end of this book include further questions specifically tailored for them.

Consider
• How do people in your political, religious, or cultural group create polarization?
• Are there ways you can help your in-group reduce polarization?
• How can you help your community heal and find common ground?

And Beyond

Some of us have the connections and ability to reduce division in community groups with relative strangers and with a wide diversity of beliefs. It may take days, weeks, or years to find common ground, but if we commit to understanding and respecting each other, these discussions can connect us, even in our differences.

---

11. Zachary Elwood, "Is Liberal Bias Impeding U.S. Depolarization and Conflict Resolution Efforts?"

Our Unique Opportunity

As Latter-day Saints, we don't self-select who we worship with, and thus our congregations provide a somewhat unique experience of living in difference. As Latter-day Saint writer McKay Coppins describes it,

> I think that one of the most radical things about Mormonism right now, and one of the great things about Mormonism, is that I have to go to church with people whose political views I abhor. I have to go to church with people who see the world entirely different from me and who have had radically different experiences from me. I not only have to sit in pews with them, but I might have to serve in presidencies with them and put on events with them and do service projects with them.[12]

Thomas Griffith, a retired Federal Judge and Latter-day Saint, shares this assessment:

> We know how to see somebody who's different than us and learn to work with them and get along with them. Now, can we take that skill that we've developed in our wards in our stakes, and can we take it out to our community? Can we be the ones in our community who are agents of reconciliation? I think we have, as Latter-day Saints, a distinctive and unique role to play at this moment.[13]

Our theology, history, and experience loving and engaging with different people give us the opportunity to lead by example in creating a community where we hear all voices and find the most common ground, even while we keep our own values. Griffith continues, "We're here to create community. We're here to create a union and that means that you need to compromise. If we listen to each other, we may learn things that will get us in a better place through the clash of ideas. Out of that will emerge better ideas, but that doesn't happen unless I'm willing to learn from you and you're willing to learn from me."[14]

Ever Outward

Right now, there are about eight billion humans living in diverse cultures. None of us, even identical twins, are the same. We have eternal,

12. Terryl Givens (host), "The Most American Religion—McKay Coppins with Terryl Givens."

13. Sarah Jane Weaver (host), "Former Federal Judge Thomas B. Griffith on the Importance of Religious Liberty and Political Civility."

14. Weaver, "Former Federal Judge Thomas B. Griffith on the Importance of Religious Liberty and Political Civility."

distinct spirits and experience life differently. We are called to be in the world, with all its differences, incivility, and acrimony. God asks us to be full of love and to show dignity to our neighbors (Matt. 7:12), the stranger (Lev. 19:33–34),[15] and those who hate us (Matt. 5:44). Our differences bring the greatest wonders and some of our biggest challenges.

The Book of Mormon teaches that as we become converted our hearts extend outward to others, including to those who have different beliefs and worldviews. Enos said his "soul hungered; and I kneeled down before my Maker, and I cried unto him in mighty prayer and supplication for mine own soul" (Enos 1:4). As he received an answer to his prayer, Enos's prayer shifted outward to "the welfare of my brethren, the Nephites; wherefore, I did pour out my whole soul unto God for them" (Enos 1:9). Finally, he expanded his group identity and "prayed unto him with many long strugglings for *my brethren*, the Lamanites" (Enos 1:11; emphasis added).[16] In this moment of heartfelt prayer, as he moved to the outer circle, the Lamanites, he set aside the antagonistic descriptions of them and instead saw them as his "brethren" and sought their welfare.

Conflict in our world dates back from the very beginning, starting with the War in Heaven and then, after the Fall, both murder and strife. The histories told in the Old Testament and the Book of Mormon open with acts of violence and detail the contrasting behaviors and mindsets that lead to either genocide or peace. Early Latter-day Saints found violence and strife in New York, Ohio, Missouri, and Nauvoo even as they sought refuge from it in Zion. The desire for peace and safety has filled prayers from the beginning. It should fill ours now.

---

15. In 2016, Relief Society General President Linda K. Burton spoke in general conference about our responsibility to help the stranger ("I Was a Stranger"). A week earlier, The Church of Jesus Christ of Latter-day Saints announced a website to help Church members find ways to help refugees. Since that time, Latter-Day Saint Charities served tens of thousands of refugees displaced by conflict in Ukraine, Syria, Afghanistan, Yemen, Ethiopia, and other countries. These initiatives are not limited to refugees but include other humanitarian efforts to help strangers among us. See the Latter-day Saint Charities website for details and their annual report.

16. Rev. Dr. Fatimah Salleh and Margaret Olsen Hemming say, "Enos' heart is expanding in this process, as evidenced by his thoughts turning gradually further outward. He describes the Lamanites as his brethren, even though they are currently in a deeply adversarial relationship . . . Enos' view is so long and his heart so compassionate that his greatest desire is for his enemies to receive help from the work of his people." Fatima Salleh and Margaret Olsen Hemming, *The Book of Mormon for the Least of These: 1 Nephi—Words of Mormon*, 136.

Just as the divine response to the Fall is the Atonement of Christ, the divine response to the conflict and violence brought on by the Fall is the Gospel of Christ. As Patrick Mason and David Pulsipher write, "peacebuilding is at the heart of the restored gospel of Jesus Christ."[17] Our Savior, the murdered Jesus, living under Roman occupation, asks us to "love your neighbor as yourself" (Mark 12:31) and "love one another; as I have loved you, that you also love one another" (John 13:34). On the night of his betrayal, he said, "Peace I leave with you, my peace I give unto you: not as the world giveth, give I unto you. Let not your heart be troubled, neither let it be afraid" (John 14:27). Then, on the cross he asked his Father to "forgive them" (Luke 23:34).

Yes, our work is hard and frustrating and full of mistakes, but its importance keeps us going. We make mistakes and get lost. Sometimes we alienate those around us and apologize, but we know we must continue. We press forward, anxiously engaged in the work of salvation for ourselves, our families, and the society in which we live today.

Whether we are members of The Church of Jesus Christ of Latter-day Saints or not, we can become what Elder Uchtdorf describes: "We can and we should be a people of peace and reconciliation. It takes empathy and action to influence the future of mankind based on dignity, honesty, and eternal values, regardless of differences in politics, religion, race, or cultural traditions."[18]

If we can do this, we ourselves change. We become bridges connecting people and ideas, helping to unify at least our bit of the world.

---

17. Patrick Q. Mason and John David Pulsipher, *Proclaim Peace: The Restoration's Answer to an Age of Conflict*, xvi.

18. Marianne Holman Prescott, "Seek and Speak Out for Peace, Elder Uchtdorf Urges During Volkstrauertag Service."

Ideas for Book Groups

You know your book group best, and you know whether it is best to discuss the book in a single sitting or to take a chapter at a time. You can use the questions at the end of each chapter or use the reflection questions throughout the chapters that particularly speak to group members. If you are a parent, consider discussing the book with your partner or other group members from your own points of view as adults, then have a separate session to brainstorm how to teach these principles to children or teens.

Start your book group with some ground rules to help everyone engage with respect and openness. Here are three simple principles I have adapted from 3Practices (check out their website). You can print these or post them visibly to highlight and reinforce them in the discussion.

- **I'll be unusually interested in others.** This means I have unusual curiosity and try to understand what others think and why they think it. I listen to understand and not to respond.

- **I'll stay in the room with difference.** If someone says something I disagree with, instead of immediately disagreeing or mentally retreating, I embrace the conversation so I can learn and grow.

- **I'll ask curious questions.** Instead of making a statement in response to someone's comment, I will be curious and ask questions so that I can better understand what they are saying. I will activate my curiosity by saying "I'd be curious to know . . ."

Any of the discussion questions in this book are suitable for personal or group reflection, but if you need more ideas, consider the following questions or make up your own. Most book groups can only discuss three to five questions in one meeting, so pick the ones that are best suited for your group.[1]

1. What chasms and divides in your life are toughest for you? Has anything in this book particularly helped you think about those opportunities?

---

1. Some of these questions are inspired by Elena Nicolaou, "The Best Book Club Questions to Spark Discussion."

2. What unique characteristics and experiences have shaped and influenced how you see the world?

3. Are you curious to better understand others' worldviews? Which ones?

4. What did you learn about bias that was helpful or disturbing?

5. What did you think about the section in chapter 5 about different faiths having different moral views? Can godly people—or even believing Latter-day Saints—have different worldviews, or is there simply right and wrong (and who decides)?

6. Can one have too much empathy? Are there dangers in spending too much time listening to what others think? Why or why not?

7. What do you think about The Utah Compromise? Is this a one-off, or do you think this is a model for other types of issues?

8. What did you learn about yourself as you read this book?

9. Which of these skills come easily to you, and which are harder for you?

10. What is the first thing you want to work on?

11. Did your opinion of this book change as you read it? If so, how?

12. If you could ask the author anything, what would it be? (Go ahead and ask me! Email **healingourdivides@gmail.com** or contact me on Facebook at **BridgesLDS**, and I'll respond when I am able.)

13. How did this book change you? What about this book do you think you'll remember in a few months or years?

14. Are there lingering questions from the book you're still thinking about?

15. Are there ways you are planning to use this book in your life or with groups around you? Where do you imagine your bridge-building journey will take you?

After the discussion, take a moment and give people an opportunity to thank others in the group for their comments or thoughtfulness. This eliminates negative feelings that come from any discussion with different opinions. This is an important part of every 3Practices discussion. You could say, "Let's end our book group by expressing thanks to people who make us think or showed curiosity or engaged with difference." Then take a moment to thank someone who did this for you. Then ask if anyone else would like to say thank you.

Resource Guide

Books

Books are a great way to explore these topics in more detail. In the "Introductory Books" category below, I list what I think is the best book in each topic area, knowing they overlap. If you want to read just one book, look at the introductory list. For more specialized information or additional insight, look to the "Additional Books" list. You can also delve deep into any of the readings and websites in the footnotes throughout this book.

Introductory Books

I Never Thought of it That Way: How to Have Fearlessly Curious Conversations in Dangerously Divided Times by Mónica Guzmán. Very accessible and light. My book uses her spheres of agreement and how to manage the setting. An easy read with practical tools.

The Righteous Mind: Why Good People Are Divided by Politics and Religion by Jonathan Haidt. Deep analysis of psychology and how it affects our religious and political beliefs. My book uses it extensively, including the analogy of the elephant and rider.

Why We're Polarized by Ezra Klein. A good political and historical analysis of the rise of polarization over the last seventy years.

Love Your Enemies: How Decent People Can Save America from the Culture of Contempt by Arthur C. Brooks. Why we need to rise above polarization and have meaningful discussions about key issues.

How Minds Change: The Surprising Science of Belief, Opinion, and Persuasion by David McRaney. He layers psychology and politics together to explain why we disagree and how to understand others and change their beliefs.

Think Again: The Power of Knowing What You Don't Know by Adam Grant. Highlights ways we can examine what we think we know so that we can more clearly see problems in our lives, relationships, and careers.

Additional Books

Proclaim Peace: The Restoration's Answer to an Age of Conflict by Patrick Q. Mason and J. David Pulsipher. Teaches how restoration doctrine and scripture includes peacemaking and nonviolent theology.

Morality: Restoring the Common Good in Divided Times by Jonathan Sacks. A theological approach to the need for and benefits of virtues and values.

Them: Why We Hate Each Other—And How to Heal by Ben Sasse. He suggests that today's polarization and contention comes from community collapse and isolation. He makes a strong case for building strong interpersonal relationships and connections.

Being Wrong: Adventures in the Margin of Error by Kathryn Schulz. Describes why we think we know things and end up being wrong.

Dignity: Its Essential Role in Resolving Conflict by Donna Hicks. Helps us understand the importance of dignity, how to recognize times when dignity is violated, and how to respond when we aren't treated with dignity.

Truth Over Tribe: Pledging Allegiance to the Lamb, Not the Donkey or the Elephant by Patrick Miller and Keith Simon. Two Christian theologians write about the Christian call to rise above tribalism using a faith-based approach.

On Being Certain: Believing You Are Right Even When You're Not by Robert A. Burton, MD. A neurologist's view of what is certainty and how we come to believe something.

Let's Talk About Hard Things by Anna Sale. Both a memoir and several stories that illustrate the importance of having hard conversations about topics including money, family, and identity.

Beyond Contempt: How Liberals Can Communicate Across the Great Divide by Erica Etelson. Although framed from a liberal perspective, everyone can learn from Eteleson's writing on how we can communicate productively and without contention.

From Politics to the Pews: How Partisanship and the Political Environment Shape Religious Identity by Michele F. Margolis. An academic analysis of the interrelationship between politics and religion. She explains how our political views shape our religious views, not the other way around.

Against Civility: The Hidden Racism in Our Obsession with Civility by Alex Zamalin. He argues, using the eighteenth century as an example, that compromises made in the name of civility have entrenched racial disparities. Makes a case that, on some issues, we shouldn't compromise in the name of civility.

Conspiracy Theories and the People Who Believe Them, edited by Joseph E. Ushinski. Compilation of experts' views to better understand today's conspiracy theories, how they arise, their effects, and what we can do about them.

Resources for Children

We want to teach our children so they know how to avoid being swept away in the worldly forces of polarization and contempt. The best way to teach children is by example. Children listen to our conversations and model how we deal with difference. If we use social or news media that foster anger, fear, or vilification, our children will model our behavior. Set the example and let them see how we overcome contention.

As parents, we can also directly teach them. We can share any of the principles in the book, but I've listed a few key foundational principles that focus on developing natural ability and skills to overcome contention.

- **Learn to listen**—Help your children learn to listen to other people and understand what others think and why. You can adapt the materials found in "Microtraining 5: How to Be an Active Listener," from *Answering My Gospel Questions (REL 280)* by the Church Educational System.

- **Become curious**—An important part of listening is to be curious and interested in others and what they think and how they live their lives. The Mayo Clinic's children's health resources offer different ways to develop a child's curiosity. We can best teach these by providing settings for them to become curious. See "8 tips to develop children's curiosity," Speaking of Health, Mayo Clinic Health System, May 15, 2020. For other resources, search online for "how to teach children to be curious."

- **Develop compassion and empathy**—As parents, we want our children to have concern for others to help them see and understand needs. See "Teaching Children Empathy" by M. Sue Bergin, *Y Magazine*, Winter 2007 or search online for "how to teach children to develop empathy."

- **Learn respect**—Respect and empathy go together. We want our children to recognize the dignity and divinity of others. The Church's website has a good resource page with talks, articles, activities, and other materials about respect. Check out "Respect" found in "Resources for Teaching Children" at www.churchofjesuschrist.org/children/resources/topics/respect.

- **Overcome in-group/out-group bias**—This is an important concept for children to learn, but it is difficult to teach. I can't find a Church-developed or secular resource about this topic for children specifically. I think it is best taught by example and in how we correct children. When we use language that refers to out-groups—like enemies, others, bad guys, etc.—we explicitly teach out-grouping. We can correct our children and give them alternative language that pulls the other person into our group. When you can't find the right language, just use *child of God*.

You can incorporate all these topics into activities and lessons. You can use *A Pattern for Growth* that includes the Discover, Plan, Act, and Reflect approach (see *Personal Development: Youth Guidebook* in the Gospel Library).

Uplift For Kids has a library of values-based lessons (www.upliftkids.org/lessons) that you can adapt to any age. Lessons that are especially applicable are Curiosity, Respect, Bullying, and Compassion.

Joining with Others

We aren't alone in this work. Even as regular people, we can get involved with existing groups. Here are a few which may be of interest. You can explore their websites and initiatives to see whether any speak to you.

- **Braver Angels**—Specifically focused on bringing conservatives and liberals together and building civic trust. They have online training programs and alliances organized in most major metropolitan areas. They can also help you set up your own to bring people together. See www.braverangels.org.

- **3Practices**—This requires no preparation or expertise. Several times a week, they host conversations on different topics, some potentially divisive. Anyone can join and take part. You can even remain completely anonymous, turn off your camera and listen in. They call these

Circles and explain a structured way to take part. It's fun and easy, and I have done dozens of these. See www.3practices.com.

- **The Listen First Coalition**—A collection of organizations focused on reducing polarization and building connections. They have their own programs and highlight the activities of others. This is a great place to start if you want to understand the breadth of groups out there; perhaps one will spark your interest. See www.listenfirstproject.org.

- **Living Room Conversations**—In these conversations, two hosts discuss an important topic. They provide guides to make these conversations useful, using many of the principles in this book. See www. livingroomconversations.org.

- **We Are Weavers**—They support practical local initiatives to accomplish specific community objectives, including a cancer survivors support group, a youth mentoring group, community revitalization, and reincorporating the incarcerated. While these initiatives are not about reducing polarization, they focus on creating engagement to accomplish something important in their community. See www.weareweavers.org.

Works Cited

"2018 Global Slavery Index." Walk Free. June 7, 2023. https://www.globalslaveryindex .org/2018/findings/global-findings/.

"The 2022 Report on How the Church of Jesus Christ Cared for Those in Need." Newsroom. The Church of Jesus Christ of Latter-day Saints. March 22, 2023. https://newsroom.churchofjesuschrist.org/article/2022-annual-report -caring-for-those-in-need.

"About." The Pluralism Project at Harvard University. Accessed December 27, 2022. https://pluralism.org/about.

Alexander, Scott (pseudonym). "I Can Tolerate Anything Except the Outgroup." Slate Star Codex. September 30, 2014. https://slatestarcodex.com/2014/09 /30/i-can-tolerate-anything-except-the-outgroup/.

"American's Support for Key LGBTQ Rights Continues to Tick Upwards, Findings from the 2021 American Values Atlas." PRRI. March 17, 2022. https:// www.prri.org/research/americans-support-for-key-lgbtq-rights-continues -to-tick-upward/.

"Areas of Focus." Templeton Religion Trust. https://templetonreligiontrust.org/areas -of-focus/.

Augsburger, David W. *Caring Enough to Hear and Be Heard*. 3rd edition. Grand Rapids: Baker Publishing Group, 2009.

Baker, Mary Ann. "Master, the Tempest is Raging." In *Hymns*. Salt Lake City: The Church of Jesus Christ of Latter-day Saints, 1985.

Ballard, M. Russell. "Children of Heavenly Father." BYU Speeches. March 3, 2020. https://speeches.byu.edu/talks/m-russell-ballard/children-heavenly-father/.

———. "Questions and Answers." BYU Speeches. November 14, 2017. https:// speeches.byu.edu/talks/m-russell-ballard/questions-and-answers/.

Bargh, J. A., and T. L. Chartrand. "The Unbearable Automaticity of Being." *American Psychologist* 54, (1990): 462–479.

Bednar, David A. "Put on Thy Strength, O Zion." The Church of Jesus Christ of Latter-day Saints. October 2022. https://www.churchofjesuschrist.org/ study/general-conference/2022/10/46bednar.

"Belonging and Boundaries—A Conversation with Jennifer Finlayson-Fife." May 23, 2021. Produced by Faith Matters podcast, episode 73. https://faithmatters. org/belonging-and-boundaries-a-conversation-with-jennifer-finlayson-fife/.

Bingham, Jean B. "I Will Bring the Light of the Gospel into My Home." The Church of Jesus Christ of Latter-day Saints. October 2016. https://www. churchofjesuschrist.org/study/ensign/2016/11/general-womens-session/i- will-bring-the-light-of-the-gospel-into-my-home.

Boghossian, Peter, and James Lindsay. *How to Have Impossible Conversations: A Very Practical Guide*. New York: Hachette Book Group, 2019.

Bourne, Greg. "What Do the Times Require?" Moving Beyond Intractability. Accessed December 27, 2022. https://www.beyondintractability.org/crq-bi-hyper-polarization-discussion/bourne-times.

Boxell, Levi, Matthew Gentzkow, and Jesse M. Shapiro. "Cross-Country Trends in Affective Polarization." National Bureau of Economic Research Working Paper Series 26669, January 2020, revised November 2021. https://www.nber.org/system/files/working_papers/w26669/w26669.pdf.

Brooks, Arthur C. *Love Your Enemies: How Decent People Can Save America from the Culture of Contempt.* New York: Harper Collins, 2019. Kindle.

———. "More Love, Less Contempt." BYU Speeches. April 25, 2019. https://speeches.byu.edu/talks/arthur-c-brooks/more-love-less-contempt/.

Brown, Matthew. "Fact check: It's true, U.S. government poisoned some alcohol during Prohibition." *USA Today.* June 23, 2020. https://www.usatoday.com/story/news/factcheck/2020/06/30/fact-check-u-s-government-poisoned-some-alcohol-during-prohibition/3283701001/.

Burgess, Guy, Heidi Burgess, and Sanda Kaufman. "Applying Conflict Resolution Insights to the Hyper-polarized, Society-wide Conflicts Threatening Liberal Democracies." *Conflict Resolution Quarterly* 39, no. 4 (March 2022): 355–69.

———. "Is liberal bias impeding U.S. depolarization and conflict resolution efforts?" *People Who Read People: A Psychology Podcast.* Transcript November 20, 2022. https://behavior-podcast.com/examining-liberal-contributions-to-american-polarization-with-guy-burgess/.

Burgess, Heidi, and Guy Burgess. "Fighting Hyper-Polarization for Our Children and Grandchildren—Newsletter 61." *Beyond Intractability.* Accessed December 27, 2022. https://beyondintractability.substack.com/p/61.

Burton, Robert A. *On Being Certain: Believing When You Are Right Even When You Are Not.* New York: St. Martin's Press, 2008. Kindle.

Cain, Fraser. "Are There More Grains of Sand Than Stars?" Universe Today. November 25, 2013. https://www.universetoday.com/106725/are-there-more-grains-of-sand-than-stars/.

Camp, Lee C. *Scandalous Witness: A Little Political Manifesto for Christians.* Grand Rapids: William B. Eerdmans, 2020.

Campbell, Carolyn. "Creating Common Ground: The Uncanny Ability of Activist Troy Williams." Good News Utah. August 17, 2022. https://goodnewsutah.com/creating-common-ground-the-uncanny-ability-of-activist-troy-williams/.

Campbell-Meiklejohn, Daniel, Arndis Simonsen, Chris D. Frith, and Nathaniel D. Daw. "Independent Neural Computation of Value from Other People's Confidence." *Journal of Neuroscience* 37, no. 3 (January 18, 2017): 673–84.

Caplan, Bryan. "The Ideological Turing Test." Econlib. Accessed January 9, 2024. https://www.econlib.org/archives/2011/06/the_ideological.html.

"Caring for Those in Need." The Church of Jesus Christ of Latter-day Saints. Last updated October 17, 2023. https://www.latterdaysaintcharities.org/.

Carroll, Lewis. *Alice in Wonderland.* Oxford: Macmillan Publishers, 1865.

Cassidy, Brittany S., Colleen Hughes, and Anne C. Krendl. "Disclosing political partisanship polarizes first impression of faces." PLOS ONE 17, no. 11 (November 9, 2022): e0276400.

Center for American Women and Politics (CAWP). "Gender Gap Public Opinion." Center for American Women and Politics, Eagleton Institute of Politics, Rutgers University–New Brunswick. 2024. https://cawp.rutgers.edu/gender -gap-public-opinion.

Chenoweth, Erica, and Jeremy Pressman, "This summer's Black Lives Matter protesters were overwhelmingly peaceful, our research finds." *The Washington Post*. October 26, 2020. https://www.washingtonpost.com/politics/2020/10/16 /this-summers-black-lives-matter-protesters-were-overwhelming-peaceful -our-research-finds/.

The Church of Jesus Christ of Latter-day Saints. "Faith." True to the Faith. https:// www.churchofjesuschrist.org/study/manual/true-to-the-faith/faith.

———. "Light of Christ." Gospel Topics. https://www.churchofjesuschrist.org/study /manual/gospel-topics/light-of-christ.

"Church Updates Temple Recommend Interview Questions." Newsroom. The Church of Jesus Christ of Latter-day Saints. October 6, 2019. https://newsroom. churchofjesuschrist.org/article/october-2019-general-conference-temple -recommend.

Clinehens, Jennifer. "The Psychological Failure of New Coke." ChoiceHacking. Accessed December 23, 2022. https://www.choicehacking.com/2022/04 /19/the-psychological-failure-of-new-coke/.

Cook, Gareth. "History and the Decline of Human Violence." Scientific American. October 4, 2011. https://www.scientificamerican.com/article/history-and -the-decline-of-human-violence/.

Cook, Quentin L. "Personal Peace in Challenging Times." The Church of Jesus Christ of Latter-day Saints. October 2021. https://www.churchofjesuschrist.org /study/general-conference/2021/10/46cook.

de Chardin, Pierre Teilhard. "Sketch of a Personal Universe." In *Human Energy*, translated by J. M. Cohen, 72. New York: Harcourt Brace Jovanovich, 1962.

"Difference and Dignity." Newsroom. The Church of Jesus Christ of Latter-day Saints. October 24, 2014. https://newsroom.churchofjesuschrist.org/article /difference-and-dignity.

"The Dignity of Human Life." Newsroom. The Church of Jesus Christ of Latter-day Saints. March 2, 2017. https://newsroom.churchofjesuschrist.org/article /the-dignity-of-human-life?__prclt=exLtgHP4.

Drutman, Lee. "How Hatred Came to Dominate American Politics." FiveThirtyEight. October 5, 2020. https://fivethirtyeight.com/features/how -hatred-negative-partisanship-came-to-dominate-american-politics/.

Elwood, Zachary. "Is Liberal Bias Impeding U.S. Depolarization and Conflict Resolution Efforts?" *People Who Read People: A Psychology Podcast*. Transcript November 20, 2022. https://behavior-podcast.com/examining-liberal- contributions-to-american-polarization-with-guy-burgess/.

Etelson, Erica. *Beyond Contempt: How Liberals Can Communicate Across the Great Divide*. Gabriola Island: New Society Publishers, 2020. Kindle.

Eubank, Sharon. "By Union of Feeling We Obtain Power with God." The Church of Jesus Christ of Latter-day Saints. October 2020. https://www .churchofjesuschrist.org/study/general-conference/2020/10/31eubank.

The European Space Agency. "How Many Stars are there in the Universe." Accessed January 5, 2023. https://www.esa.int/Science_Exploration/Space_Science/ Herschel/How_many_stars_are_there_in_the_Universe.

Evers-Hillstrom, Karl. "Most Expensive Ever: 2020 Election Cost $14.4 Billion." Open Secrets. February 22, 2021. https://www.opensecrets.org/news/2021 /02/2020-cycle-cost-14p4-billion-doubling-16/.

"The Family: A Proclamation to the World." The Church of Jesus Christ of Latter-day Saints. https://www.churchofjesuschrist.org/study/scriptures/ the-family-a-proclamation-to-the-world/the-family-a-proclamation-to -the-world.

"The First Presidency Urges Latter-day Saints to Wear Face Masks When Needed and Get Vaccinated Against COVID-19." First Presidency Message. The Church of Jesus Christ of Latter-day Saints. August 21, 2021. https:// newsroom.churchofjesuschrist.org/article/first-presidency-message-covid -19-august-2021.

Frazer, S., A. El-Shafei, and A. M. Gill. *Reality Check: Being Nonreligious in America*. Cranford: American Atheists, 2020.

Frimer, Jeremy, Harinder Aujla, Matthew Feinberg, Linda Skitka, Karl Aquino, Johannes C. Eichstaedt, and Robb Willer. "Incivility is Rising among American Politicians on Twitter." *Social Psychological and Personality Science* 14, no. 2 (April 28, 2022).

"Garments." Gospel Topics. The Church of Jesus Christ of Latter-day Saints. https:// www.churchofjesuschrist.org/study/manual/gospel-topics/garments.

Geisel, Theodor Seuss (Dr. Seuss). *The Lorax*. New York: Random House, 1971.

Gilbert, Scott F., Anna L. Tyler, and Emily Zackin. *Bioethics and the New Embryology: Springboard for Debate*. New York: W. H. Freeman and Sinauer Associates, 2005.

Givens, Terryl (host). "The Most American Religion—McKay Coppins with Terryl Givens." December 28, 2020. Produced by Faith Matters podcast, episode 56. https: //podcasts.apple.com/us/podcast/56-the-most-american-religion-mckay- coppins-with/id1307757928?i=1000503680444.

Givens, Terryl, and Fiona Givens. *The God Who Weeps: How Mormonism Makes Sense of Life*. Crawfordsville: R. R. Donnelley, 2012.

Gottman, John M. *The Science of Trust: Emotional Attunement for Couples*. New York: W. W. Norton, 2011.

Grant, Adam (@AdamMGrant). "Changing your mind is not a sign of losing integrity." Twitter post, November 27, 2022. https://twitter.com/ AdamMGrant/status/1596915049129459716.

———. "We pay too much attention to the most confident voices." Twitter post, December 9, 2022. https://twitter.com/AdamMGrant/status /1601257372483059713.

Gray, Alison J. "Worldviews." *International Psychiatry* 8, no. 3 (August 1, 2011): 58–60.

Green, Marc. "Driver Reaction Time." Marc Green PhD Human Factors. Accessed December 23, 2022. https://www.visualexpert.com/Resources/reactiontime.html.

Greenberg, Irving. "Covenantal Pluralism." *Journal of Ecumenical Studies* 34, no. 3 (Summer 1997): 427.

Grow, Lisa. "'The Great Check': Reflections on Disaster and Faith." In *Every Needful Thing: Essays on the Life of the Mind and Heart,* edited by Melissa Wei-Tsing Inouye and Kate Holbrook. Salt Lake City: Deseret Book, 2023.

Guzmán, Mónica. *I Never Thought of It That Way: How to Have Fearlessly Curious Conversations in Dangerously Divided Times.* Dallas: BenBella Books, 2022.

Haidt, Jonathan. *The Righteous Mind: Why Good People Are Divided by Politics and Religion.* New York: Vintage Books, 2012.

Hallin, Dallin G. *The Uncensored War, The Media and Vietnam.* New York: Oxford University Press, 1986.

Hao, Karen. "The Facebook Whistleblower Says Its Algorithms Are Dangerous. Here's Why." MIT Technology Review. October 5, 2021. https://www.technologyreview.com/2021/10/05/1036519/facebook-whistleblower -frances-haugen-algorithms/.

———. "YouTube Is Experimenting with Ways to Make Its Algorithm Even More Addictive." MIT Technology Review. September 27, 2019. https://www.technologyreview.com/2019/09/27/132829/youtube-algorithm-gets -more-addictive/.

Hatemi, Peter K., Sarah E. Medland, Robert Klemmensen, Sven Oskarrson, Levente Littvay, Chris Dawes, Brad Verhulst, Rose McDermott, Asbjørn Sonne Nørgaard, Casey Klofstad, Kaare Christensen, Magnus Johannesson, Patrik K. E. Magnusson, Lindon J. Eaves, and Nicholas G. Martin, "Genetic Influences on Political Ideologies: Twin Analyses of 19 Measures of Political Ideologies from Five Democracies and Genome-Wide Findings from Three Populations." *Behavior Genetics* 44, no. 3 (May 2014): 282–294.

Hensley, Scott. "Poll: Americans Say We're Angrier Than a Generation Ago." NPR. June 26, 2019. https://www.npr.org/sections/health-shots/2019/06/26 /735757156/poll-americans-say-were-angrier-than-a-generation-ago.

Hicks, Donna. *Dignity: Its Essential Role in Resolving Conflict.* New Haven: Yale University Press: 2021.

Hinckley, Gordon B. "The Healing Power of Christ." The Church of Jesus Christ of Latter-day Saints. November 1988. https://www.churchofjesuschrist.org /study/general-conference/1988/10/the-healing-power-of-christ.

———. *Stand a Little Taller.* Salt Lake City: Deseret Book, 2001.

Holland, Jeffrey R. "Lord, I Believe." The Church of Jesus Christ of Latter-day Saints. April 2013. https://www.churchofjesuschrist.org/study/general-conference /2013/04/lord-i-believe.

———. "A Perfect Brightness of Hope." The Church of Jesus Christ of Latter-day Saints. April 2020. https://www.churchofjesuschrist.org/study/general-conference /2020/04/43holland.

Horwitz, Jeff, and Deepa Seetharaman. "Facebook Executives Shut Down Efforts to Make the Site Less Divisive." *Wall Street Journal.* May 26, 2022. https://www.wsj.com/articles/facebook-knows-it-encourages-division-top-executives-nixed-solutions-11590507499.

Housel, Morgan. *The Psychology of Money: Timeless Lessons on Wealth, Greed, and Happiness.* Petersfield: Harriman House LTD, 2020.

Hudson, Valerie M. "The Two-Way Street of Faith and Scholarship: A Political Scientist's Experience." In *Every Needful Thing: Essays on the Life of the Mind and the Heart*, edited by Melissa Wei-Tsing Inouye and Kate Holbrook. Salt Lake City: Deseret Book, 2023.

Hunter, Howard W. "A More Excellent Way." The Church of Jesus Christ of Latter-day Saints. April 1992. https://www.churchofjesuschrist.org/study/general-conference/1992/04/a-more-excellent-way.

Inouye, Melissa Wei-Tsing, and Kate Holbrook, ed. *Every Needful Thing: Essays on the Life of the Mind and Heart.* Salt Lake City: Deseret Book, 2023.

"Invite Diligent Learning." *Teaching in the Savior's Way: For All Who Teach in the Home and in the Church.* The Church of Jesus Christ of Latter-day Saints. June 8, 2022. https://www.churchofjesuschrist.org/study/manual/teaching-in-the-saviors-way-2022/07-part-2/11-invite-diligent-learning.

Jensen, Marlin K. "To Walk Humbly with Thy God." The Church of Jesus Christ of Latter-day Saints. April 2001. https://www.churchofjesuschrist.org/study/general-conference/2001/04/to-walk-humbly-with-thy-god.

Jensen, Ryan. "In Valentine's Day message, President Nelson asks for an increase in 'lovingkindness.'" *Church News.* February 14, 2022. https://www.thechurchnews.com/2022/2/14/23216525/president-nelson-valentines-day-message-lovingkindness.

Joseph Smith History, 1838–1856, volume E-1, created 1 July 1843–30 April 1844, p. 1680. *The Joseph Smith Papers.* Accessed December 23, 2022. https://www.josephsmithpapers.org/paper-summary/history-1838-1856-volume-e-1-1-july-1843-30-april-1844/50.

Journal of Discourses. 26 vols. London: LDS Booksellers Depot, 1874.

"Judaism and Abortion." National Council of Jewish Women. Accessed February 27, 2023. https://www.ncjw.org/wp-content/uploads/2019/05/Judaism-and-Abortion-FINAL.pdf.

Kapp, Ardeth G. "Young Women Striving Together." The Church of Jesus Christ of Latter-day Saints. October 1984. https://www.churchofjesuschrist.org/study/general-conference/1984/10/young-women-striving-together.

Kenney, Robert F. "Day of Affirmation Address." John F. Kennedy Presidential Library and Museum. June 6, 1966. https://www.jfklibrary.org/learn/about-jfk/the-kennedy-family/robert-f-kennedy/robert-f-kennedy-speeches/day-of-affirmation-address-university-of-capetown-capetown-south-africa-june-6-1966.

King, Martin Luther, Jr. "Where Do We Go From Here?" Address to Southern Christian Leadership Conference, Atlanta. August 16, 1967. https://kinginstitute.stanford.edu/where-do-we-go-here.

Klein, Ezra. "The Single Most Important Fact About American Politics." Vox. April 28, 2016. https://www.vox.com/2014/6/13/5803768 /pew-most-important-fact-american-politics.

———. *Why We're Polarized*. New York: Avid Reader Press, 2020.

Kleinfeld, Rachel. "The Rise in Political Violence in the United State and Damage to Our Democracy." Testimony before the Select Committee to Investigate the January 6th Attack on the United States Capitol. March 31, 2022. Published by the Carnegie Endowment for International Peace. https:// carnegieendowment.org/2022/03/31/rise-in-political-violence-in-united-states-and-damage-to-our-democracy-pub-87584.

Kruger, Justin, and David Dunning, "Unskilled and unaware of it: how difficulties in recognizing one's own incompetence lead to inflated self-assessments." *Journal of Personal and Social Psychology* 77, no. 6 (December 1999): 1121–34.

Lathrap, Mary T. "Walk a Mile in His Moccasins." AAA Native Arts. Modified May 1, 2014. https://www.aaanativearts.com/walk-mile-in-his-moccasins.

"Legislation should not polarize religious liberties, anti-discrimination protections." *Deseret News*. April 4, 2015. https://www.deseret.com/2015/4/4/20562022 /legislation-should-not-polarize-religious-liberties-anti-discrimination-protections.

Lewis, Robert. "Westboro Baptist Church." Britannica. Accessed January 13, 2022. https://www.britannica.com/topic/Westboro-Baptist-Church.

"Line Upon Line: Doctrine and Covenants 121:41–43." *New Era*. The Church of Jesus Christ of Latter-day Saints. June 2011. https://www.churchofjesuschrist .org/study/new-era/2011/06/doctrine-and-covenants-121-41-43.

Lord, Charles G., Mark R. Lepper, and Elizabeth Preston. "Considering the Opposite: A Corrective Strategy for Social Judgment." *Journal of Personality and Social Psychology* 47, no. 6 (1984): 1231–43.

Mari, Silvia, Homero Gil de Zúñiga, Ahmet Suerdem, Katja Hanke, Gary Brown, Roosevelt Vilar, Diana Boer, and Michal Bilewicz. "Conspiracy Theories and Institutional Trust: Examining the Role of Uncertainty Avoidance and Active Social Media Use." *Political Psychology* 43, no. 2 (May 14, 2021): 277–96.

Masigan, Andrew J. "TikTok's 'Secret Sauce': Numbers Don't Lie." Business World. October 23, 2022. https://www.bworldonline.com/opinion/2022/10/23 /482240/tiktoks-secret-sauce/.

Mason, Patrick Q., and J. David Pulsipher. *Proclaim Peace: The Restoration's Answer to an Age of Conflict*. Provo: Neal A. Maxwell Institute for Religious Scholarship and Deseret Book, 2021.

McLaren, Brian. "Learning How to See, Recognizing Our Biases." Daily Meditations. Center for Action and Contemplation. March 1, 2021.

McNeill, Donald P., Douglas A. Morrison, and Henri J. M. Nouwen. *Compassion: A Reflection on the Christian Life*. New York: Image Books, 1983.

McRaney, David. *How Minds Change: The Surprising Science of Belief, Opinion, and Persuasion*. New York: Penguin Random House, 2022. Kindle.

Merriam-Webster.com Dictionary. "Whataboutism." Accessed March 15, 2023. https://www.merriam-webster.com/dictionary/whataboutism.

"Microtraining 5: How to Be an Active Listener." Answering My Gospel Questions Teacher Material (Religion 280). The Church of Jesus Christ of Latter-day Saints. 2022. https://www.churchofjesuschrist.org/study/manual/answering -my-gospel-questions-teacher-material/4-appendix-a/21-microtraining-5.

Miller, Patrick, and Keith Simon. *Truth over Tribe: Pledging Allegiance to the Lamb, Not the Donkey or the Elephant*. Colorado Springs: David C. Cook, 2022.

"Modeling the Future of Religion in America, How U.S. Religious Composition Has Changed in Recent Decades." Pew Research Center. September 13, 2022. https://www.pewresearch.org/religion/2022/09/13/how-u-s-religious -composition-has-changed-in-recent-decades/.

"Modeling the Future of Religion in America, If Recent Trends in Religious Switching Continue, Christians Could Make up Less than Half of the U.S. Population Within a Few Decades." Pew Research Center. September 13, 2022. https://www.pewresearch.org/religion/2022/09/13/modeling-the-future -of-religion-in-america/.

Molenberghs, Pascal, Guy Prochilo, Niklas K. Steffens, Hannes Zacher, and S. Alexander Haslam. "The Neuroscience of Inspirational Leadership: The Importance of Collective-Oriented Language and Shared Group membership." *Journal of Management* 43, no. 7 (September 2017): 2190.

Monson, Thomas S. "Until We Meet Again." The Church of Jesus Christ of Latter-day Saints. October 2008. https://www.churchofjesuschrist.org/study /general-conference/2014/04/until-we-meet-again.

Moore, Beth (@BethMooreLPM). "Thing is, we have to really be careful about who we hate." Twitter post, August 15, 2022. https://x.com/bethmoorelpm/status /1559221915973308416?s=46&t=s6z8vnzucTSRvPS8BoSoQw.

Morin, Rich. "Study on Twins Suggests Our Political Beliefs May Be Hard-Wired." Pew Research Center. December 9, 2013. https://www.pewresearch.org/ short-reads/2013/12/09/study-on-twins-suggests-our-political-beliefs-may -be-hard-wired/.

Movement Advancement Project. "Talking about Religious Exemption Laws." Arcus Foundation. December 15, 2015. https://www.arcusfoundation.org/wp -content/uploads/2015/12/talking-about-religious-exemptions-laws.pdf.

"Moving from Tolerance to Pluralism." Templeton Religion Trust. https:// templetonreligiontrust.org/covenantal-pluralism/.

"My Baptismal Covenants." The Church of Jesus Christ of Latter-day Saints. Accessed January 13, 2023. https://www.churchofjesuschrist.org/bc/content/shared/ content/images/gospel-library/manual/34594_000_014_02-covenants.pdf.

Napier, Nancy K. "The Myth of Multitasking: Think you can multitask well? Think again." Psychology Today. May 12, 2014. https://www.psychologytoday.com /us/blog/creativity-without-borders/201405/the-myth-of-multitasking.

Nelson, Russell M. "Choices for Eternity." The Church of Jesus Christ of Latter-day Saints. May 15, 2022. https://www.churchofjesuschrist.org/study /broadcasts/worldwide-devotional-for-young-adults/2022/05/12nelson.

———. "Let God Prevail." The Church of Jesus Christ of Latter-day Saints. October 2020. https://www.churchofjesuschrist.org/study/general-conference/2020 /10/46nelson.

———. "Peacemakers Needed." The Church of Jesus Christ of Latter-Day Saints. April 2023. https://www.churchofjesuschrist.org/study/general-conference/2023 /04/47nelson.

———. "Preaching the Gospel of Peace." The Church of Jesus Christ of Latter-day Saints. April 2022. https://www.churchofjesuschrist.org/study/general -conference/2022/04/11nelson.

Newberry, Christina. "How the Facebook Algorithm Works in 2023 and How to Make it Work for You." Hootsuite. Accessed December 26, 2022.

"A New Mission for Latter-day Saints—Peacemaking." *Mormon Land*. Transcript November 2, 2023. https://www.patreon.com/posts/full-episode-new -92133834.

Newell, Lloyd D. "'All Are Alike unto God': Equality and Charity in the Book of Mormon." In *Living the Book of Mormon: Abiding by Its Precepts*, edited by Gaye Strathearn and Charles Swift. Provo: Religious Studies Center, Brigham Young University; Salt Lake City: Deseret Book, 2007.

Nichols, Ralph G. *Are You Listening*. New York: McGraw Hill Book Company, 1957.

Nickerson, Charlotte. "Understanding Accommodation and Assimilation in Psychology." Simply Psychology. December 3, 2021. https://www .simplypsychology.org/what-is-accommodation-and-assimilation.html.

Nicolaou, Elena. "The Best Book Club Questions to Spark Discussion." Oprah Daily. February 28, 2020. https://www.oprahdaily.com/entertainment/a31047508 /book-club-questions/.

Oaks, Dallin H. "Going Forward with Religious Freedom and Nondiscrimination." Newsroom. The Church of Jesus Christ of Latter-day Saints. November 12, 2021. https://newsroom.churchofjesuschrist.org/article/president-dallin-h-oaks -speech-university-of-virginia.

———. "Love Your Enemies." The Church of Jesus Christ of Latter-day Saints. October 2020. https://www.churchofjesuschrist.org/study/general-conference/2020 /10/17oaks.

———. "Opposition in All Things." The Church of Jesus Christ of Latter-day Saints. April 2016. https://www.churchofjesuschrist.org/study/general-conference /2016/04/opposition-in-all-things.

Oeberst, Aileen, and Roland Imhoff. "Toward Parsimony in Bias Research: A Proposed Common Framework of Belief-Consistent Information Processing for a Set of Biases." *Perspectives on Psychological Science* 18, no. 6 (March 17, 2023): 1464–87.

Olsen, Billie. "LGBTQ+ Terms to Avoid and What to Use Instead." LGBTQ and All. October 2, 2021. https://www.lgbtqandall.com/lgbtq-terms-to-avoid -and-what-to-use-instead/.

Olson, Eric T. "Personal Identity." Stanford Encyclopedia of Philosophy. August 20, 2002, substantive revision September 6, 2019, accessed December 23, 2022. https://plato.stanford.edu/entries/identity-personal/.

Oscarson, Bonnie L. "Sisterhood: Oh, How We Need Each Other." The Church of Jesus Christ of Latter-day Saints. April 2014. https://www.churchofjesuschrist .org/study/general-conference/2014/04/sisterhood-oh-how-we-need-each-other.

Ostler, Blaire. *Queer Mormon Theology: An Introduction.* Newburgh: By Common Consent Press, 2021.

Ostler, David. *Bridges: Ministering to Those Who Question.* 2nd edition. Draper: Greg Kofford Books, 2022.

Oxford Learner's Dictionaries. "Cognition." Accessed December 23, 2022. https:// www.oxfordlearnersdictionaries.com/us/definition/english/cognition.

Patterson, Robert E., and Robert G. Eggleston, "Intuitive Cognition." *Journal of Cognitive Engineering and Decision Making* 11, no. 1 (2017): 5–22.

Pew Research Center. "Partisan Antipathy: More Intense, More Personal." October 10, 2019. https://www.pewresearch.org/politics/2019/10/10/partisan-antipathy -more-intense-more-personal/.

Preach My Gospel. Salt Lake City: The Church of Jesus Christ of Latter-day Saints, 2004.

Prescott, Marianne Holman. "Seek and Speak Out for Peace, Elder Uchtdorf Urges During Volkstrauertag Service." *Church News.* November 19, 2018. https:// www.churchofjesuschrist.org/church/news/seek-and-speak-out-for-peace-elder-uchtdorf-urges-during-volkstrauertag-service.

PRRI Staff. "Abortion Attitudes in a Post-Roe World: Findings From the 50-State 2022 American Values Atlas." PRRI. February 23, 2023. https://www.prri. org/research/abortion-attitudes-in-a-post-roe-world-findings-from-the-50-state-2022-american-values-atlas/.

"Punta del Este Declaration on Human Dignity for Everyone Everywhere: Seventy Years after the Universal Declaration of Human Rights." December 2018. https:// classic.iclrs.org/content/blurb/files/Punta%20del%20Este%20Declaration .pdf.

Renlund, Dale G. "Infuriating Unfairness." The Church of Jesus Christ of Latter-day Saints. April 2021. https://www.churchofjesuschrist.org/study/general -conference/2021/04/25renlund.

———. "The Peace of Christ Abolishes Enmity." The Church of Jesus Christ of Latter-Day Saints. October 2021. https://www.churchofjesuschrist.org/study /general-conference/2021/10/43renlund.

Reuters Staff. "Fact Check: Evidence Disproves Claims of Italian Conspiracy to Meddle in U.S. Election (Known as #ItalyGate)." Reuters. January 15, 2021. https://www.reuters.com/article/idUSKBN29K2MY/.

Riess, Jana. *The Next Mormons: How Millennials Are Changing the LDS Church.* New York: Oxford University Press, 2019.

———. "Younger US Mormons Voted for Biden, but Trump Performed Well Overall." Religion News. April 1, 2021. https://religionnews.com/2021/04/01/younger -u-s-mormons-voted-for-biden-but-trump-performed-well-overall/.

Rohr, Richard. "Following Jesus' Way." Richard Rohr's Daily Mediation. The Center for Action and Contemplation. February 19, 2023. https://cac.org /daily-meditations/following-jesus-way-2023-02-19/.

rozzzafly. "Surprised Kitty (Original)." October 13, 2009. YouTube video. https:// www.youtube.com/watch?v=0Bmhjf0rKe8.

Ryota, Kanai, Tom Feilden, Colin Firth, and Geraint Rees. "Political Orientations Are Correlated with Brain Structure in Young Adults." *Current Biology* 21, no. 8 (April 26, 2011): 670–680.

Sacks, Jonathan. "Listen, Really Listen." Aish. Accessed December 26, 2022. https:// aish.com/489453701/.

———. *Morality*. New York City, Basic Books: 2020. Kindle.

Salleh, Fatima, and Margaret Olsen Hemming. *The Book of Mormon for the Least of These: 1 Nephi—Words of Mormon*. Salt Lake City, By Common Consent Press: 2020.

Schleifer, David, Will Friedman, and Erin McNally. "Putting Partisan Animosity in Perspective: A Hidden Common Ground Report." Public Agenda. November 2021. https://publicagenda.org/wp-content/uploads/Putting-Partisan-Animosity -in-Perspective-REPORT-Final-2.pdf.

Shakespeare, William. *As You Like It*.

Sherkat, Darren E. *Changing Faith: The Dynamics and Consequences of Americans' Shifting Religious Identities*. New York City: New York University Press, 2014.

Shihab, Alwi. "Building Bridges to Harmony Through Understanding." BYU Speeches. October 10, 2006. https://speeches.byu.edu/talks /alwi-shihab/building-bridges-harmony-understanding/.

Soares, Ulisses. "Foundations and Fruits of Religious Freedom." Newsroom. The Church of Jesus Christ of Latter-day Saints. October 28, 2020. https:// newsroom.churchofjesuschrist.org/article/elder-soares-foundations -fruits-religious-freedom.

"Statement from President Biden on Marijuana Reform." The White House. October 6, 2022. https://www.whitehouse.gov/briefing-room/statements-releases/2022/10 /06/statement-from-president-biden-on-marijuana-reform/.

Statista Research Department. "Advertising Revenues Generated by Facebook Worldwide from 2017 to 2026." Statista. July 27, 2022. https://www.statista.com/statistics/544001/facebooks-advertising -revenue-worldwide-usa/.

Stefon, Matt. "Fairness Doctrine, United States Policy [1949–1987]." Britannica Online. Accessed December 26, 2022. https://www.britannica.com /topic/Fairness-Doctrine.

Stevenson, Gary E. "Love, Share, Invite." The Church of Jesus Christ of Latter-day Saints. April 2022. https://www.churchofjesuschrist.org/study/general -conference/2022/04/43stevenson.

Stewart, W. Christopher, Chris Seiple, and Dennis R. Hoover. "Toward a Global Covenant of Peaceable Neighborhood: Introducing the Philosophy of Covenantal Pluralism." *The Review of Faith & International Affairs* 18, no. 4 (2020): 1–17.

Studious Guy. "9 Dunning-Kruger Effect Examples in Real Life." Accessed December 26, 2022. https://studiousguy.com/dunning-kruger-effect -examples-in-real-life/.

Tanner, Susan W. "I Am the Light Which Ye Shall Hold Up." The Church of Jesus Christ of Latter-day Saints. April 2006. https://www.churchofjesuschrist .org/study/general-conference/2006/04/i-am-the-light-which-ye-shall -hold-up.

Teachings of the Presidents of the Church: Heber J. Grant. Salt Lake City: The Church of Jesus Christ of Latter-day Saints, 2002.

"Temple Ordinances for the Living." General Handbook: Serving in The Church of Jesus Christ of Latter-day Saints. The Church of Jesus Christ of Latter-day Saints. August 2022. https://www.churchofjesuschrist.org /study/manual/general-handbook/27-temple-ordinances-for-the-living #title_number11.

"Temples." Newsroom. The Church of Jesus Christ of Latter-day Saints. https:// newsroom.churchofjesuschrist.org/topic/temples.

Templeton, John. *Possibility for Over One Hundredfold More Spiritual Information: The Humble Approach in Theology and Science.* West Conshohocken: Templeton Press, 2000.

Uchtdorf, Dieter F. "Acting on the Truths of the Gospel of Jesus Christ," Worldwide Leadership Training, The Church of Jesus Christ of Latter-day Saints. January 2012. https://www.churchofjesuschrist.org/study/video/ worldwide-leadership-training/2012/2012-02-1050-acting-on-the-truths -of-the-gospel-of-jesus-christ.

———. "Bearers of Heavenly Light." The Church of Jesus Christ of Latter-day Saints. October 2017. https://www.churchofjesuschrist.org/study/general-conference /2017/10/bearers-of-heavenly-light.

———. "Come, Join with Us." The Church of Jesus Christ of Latter-day Saints. October 2013. https://www.churchofjesuschrist.org/study/general-conference /2013/10/come-join-with-us.

———. "Four Titles." The Church of Jesus Christ of Latter-Day Saints. April 2013. https://www.churchofjesuschrist.org/study/general-conference/2013 /04/four-titles.

———. "What Is Truth?" BYU Speeches. January 14, 2013. https://speeches.byu .edu/talks/dieter-f-uchtdorf/what-is-truth/.

Uscinski, Joseph E. *Conspiracy Theories and the People Who Believe Them.* New York: Oxford University Press, 2019. Kindle.

Vogels, Emily A., Risa Gelles-Watnick, and Navid Massara. "Teens, Social Media and Technology 2022." Pew Research Center. August 10, 2022. https://www.pewresearch.org/internet/2022/08/10/teens-social -media-and-technology-2022/.

Wagner, Michael W., Dona-Gene Mitchell, and Elizabeth Theiss-Morse. "The Consequences of Political Vilification." Paper presented at the annual meeting of the American Political Science Association, Seattle. September 1–4, 2011.

Walker, Sydney. "Watch: Be Cautious in Seeking Truth, President Oaks Says in New Video." *Church News.* February 1, 2021. https://www.thechurchnews. com/2021/2/1/23218150/in-search-of-truth-video-president-oaks.

Watson, Julie. "Comparison between Capitol siege, BLM protests is denounced." *AP News.* January 14, 2021. https://apnews.com/article/donald-trump -capitol-siege-race-and-ethnicity-violence-racial-injustice-afd7dc2165f 355a3e6dc4e9418019eb5.

Weaver, Sarah Jane (host). "Former Federal Judge Thomas B. Griffith on the Importance of Religious Liberty and Political Civility." August 30, 2022. Produced by *Church News* podcast, episode 99. https://www. thechurchnews.com/podcast/2022/8/30/23328940/episode-99-former -federal-judge-thomas-b-griffith-importance-of-religious-liberty -political-civility.

Weber Shandwick. "Civility in America 2019: Solutions for Tomorrow." Powell Tate, KRC Research. June 16, 2019. https://webershandwick.com /news/civility-in-america-2019-solutions-for-tomorrow.

Index

Also available from
GREG KOFFORD BOOKS

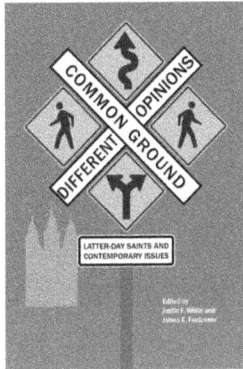

Common Ground—Different Opinions:
Latter-day Saints and Contemporary Issues

Edited by Justin F. White
and James E. Faulconer

Paperback, ISBN: 978-1-58958-573-7

There are many hotly debated issues about which many people disagree, and where common ground is hard to find. From evolution to environmentalism, war and peace to political partisanship, stem cell research to same-sex marriage, how we think about controversial issues affects how we interact as Latter-day Saints.

In this volume various Latter-day Saint authors address these and other issues from differing points of view. Though they differ on these tough questions, they have all found common ground in the gospel of Jesus Christ and the latter-day restoration. Their insights offer diverse points of view while demonstrating we can still love those with whom we disagree.

Praise for *Common Ground—Different Opinions*:

"[This book] provide models of faithful and diverse Latter-day Saints who remain united in the body of Christ. This collection clearly demonstrates that a variety of perspectives on a number of sensitive issues do in fact exist in the Church. . . . [T]he collection is successful in any case where it manages to give readers pause with regard to an issue they've been fond of debating, or convinces them to approach such conversations with greater charity and much more patience. It served as just such a reminder and encouragement to me, and for that reason above all, I recommend this book." — Blair Hodges, Maxwell Institute

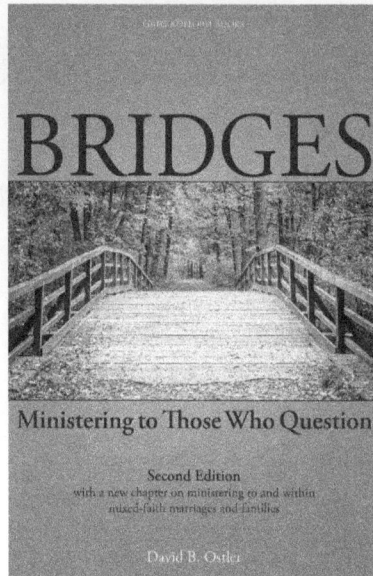

Praise for *Bridges: Ministering to Those Who Question*

"A deeply Christian book that calls upon us all to seek understanding and minister to the wounded."

—Terryl Givens, co-author of *The Crucible of Doubt: Reflections on the Quest for Faith*

"Honest, compassionate, and inspiring. . . . [Latter-day Saints] would be well-served to have a dog-eared copy of Bridges in every ward and stake council member's home."

—Patrick Q. Mason, author of *Planted: Belief and Belonging in an Age of Doubt*

"Bridges is a book that every Church leader and parent should read."

—*The Millennial Star*

"A helpful and insightful resource for anyone wondering how to respond appropriately, kindly and compassionately to loved ones who are questioning their faith."

—*Deseret News*

"One of the most important books I have read in the past decade."

—Robert A. Rees, Co-founder and Vice-President, Bountiful Children's Foundation

"I encourage you to read this book ... and then forward the book ... to members in your circle of influence and encourage them to do the same."

—*Exponent II*

www.ingramcontent.com/pod-product-compliance
Lightning Source LLC
Chambersburg PA
CBHW021401090426
42742CB00009B/947